D1134505

THE NATIONAL TRUST BOOK OF
Traditional Puddings

Sara Paston-Williams

DAVID & CHARLES
Newton Abbot   London   North Pomfret (Vt)

British Library Cataloguing in Publication Data

Paston-Williams, Sara
    The National Trust book of traditional puddings.
    1. Desserts
    I. Title
    641.8′6   TX773

    ISBN 0–7153–8451–1

First published 1983
Second impression 1986

Typeset by ABM Typographics Limited, Hull
and printed in Great Britain
by Redwood Burn Limited, Trowbridge, Wilts
for David & Charles Publishers plc
Brunel House   Newton Abbot   Devon

Published in the United States of America
by David & Charles Inc
North Pomfret   Vermont 05053   USA

CONTENTS

For all pudding lovers

With thanks to my mother and father
for trying out some of the recipes,
and to my husband and friends
who willingly put their figures at risk
by tasting the following puddings.
Grateful thanks also to Pat Richards
for devoting so much of her precious time
to typing the manuscript.

INTRODUCTION

Blessed be he that invented pudding! For it is manna that hits
the palates of all sortes of people, better even than that of the
wilderness. Ah! what an excellent thing is an English pudding!
To come in pudding-time is as much as to say to come in the
most lucky moment in the world.

This was written by a Monsieur Misson de Valbourg, a French visitor
to Britain in 1690. Another visitor, an Italian, around the same time
wrote home saying 'English pies and puddings are literally stuffed
with dried fruits and no-one who has not seen it with his own eyes
could possibly believe what an incredible number of such pies and
puddings the average Englishman is capable of eating!'

The British tradition for delicious puddings is not only centuries
old but almost unique. The wide range of sweet foods available is un-
surpassed. Puddings, pies, trifles, tansies, fools, flummeries, betties,
moulds and tarts have all been served regularly since early medieval
times. From the earliest medieval recipes, through elaborate and
brilliant Elizabethan and Stuart confections to the elegant
eighteenth- and substantial nineteenth-century puddings, a tradition
has evolved which is an integral part of Britain's culinary heritage.

Almost all British puddings (and here, as in the rest of the book, I
am using the word to describe any dish served at the sweet course)
have descended from two medieval dishes: the early cereal 'pottage',
which was a kind of porridge with honey, wild fruits and shredded
meat or fish added to make it more palatable, and 'frumenty', a milk
pudding made from wheat or barley eaten with milk and honey on
festive occasions. Originally, puddings such as brightly coloured
spiced jellies, flummeries, syllabubs, various tarts, custards, junkets
and fruit dishes formed part of a second or third course of a meal,
served alongside chicken and fish dishes. A typical second course
might consist of veal, sweetbreads, lobster, apricot tart and, in the
middle of the table, a pyramid of syllabubs and jellies. Later, a
'banquet' or sweetmeat course was introduced and the dishes became
increasingly elaborate and rich, with eggs and cream. The
Elizabethans' love of sugar is well known and this love has continued
to the present day. Our fondness for jam, honey and treacle is com-
parable only to that of some of the eastern peoples.

The enormous variety of puddings and the amazing rapidity with

5

which they were developed in the seventeenth and eighteenth centuries show that they filled a real need in the British people's diet, in humble homes as well as wealthy. Rich in fat and carbohydrates to keep out the cold, and in sugar and fruit to build up energy, the Englishman's pudding filled his stomach and satisfied his appetite. The puddings of country folk were often made from meal of cheaper local grains such as oats and barley rather than wheat, but they were just as satisfying.

British cooking has always been influenced by its monarchs and our puddings are no exception. George I was known as 'Pudding George' and is probably the Georgie Porgie mentioned in the well-known nursery rhyme! He, followed by George II and III, loved fattening, suety, German boiled puddings and dumplings which were devoured all over the kingdom. It was quite common to see plum duffs and

currant dumplings sold in the streets of London for a halfpenny each.

With the French Revolution came a great transformation in British cooking. Many French chefs fled to Britain and a change of fashion in court circles resulted in the vogue for employing them. Queen Victoria employed a number of French chefs, the most famous being Francatelli, who created puddings which we still know today — Queen's Pudding, Her Majesty's Pudding, Empress Pudding and Albert Pudding. One famous chef who worked for Napoleon I was lured to Britain to work for the Prince Regent whose interest in food is well known. This fashion was soon copied by a growing and increasingly prosperous middle class who, socially aspiring, encouraged their cooks to make French dishes or, failing that, simply to give traditional British ones French names. Many of the most delicious and subtle puddings of Georgian days were temporarily forgotten, and the rather heavy nursery-style puddings of Victorian times influenced by Prince Albert and his German habits became popular.

The new literacy of the Georgian era had a tremendous influence on

6

cookery. It allowed people, especially women, to write down their favourite recipes, and regional dishes were mentioned. Many of the traditional pudding recipes remained and were preserved in rural areas, particularly in the country houses and manors. In the towns, speciality restaurants, gentlemen's clubs and grill rooms of the more exclusive hotels continued to serve only truly British puddings and many of these have survived, although not always in their original form. There is hardly a town in Britain that does not have a local pud! In recent years, British food has enjoyed a well-deserved revival with more and more hotels and restaurants serving our great national dishes and regional specialities. Puddings are a great attraction. Although some are inclined to be rich and fattening, they are homely and delicious and make a lovely treat for the family. Most people, especially men, seem to react very favourably to such puds as Spotted Dick, Treacle Duff, Golden Pudding and Treacle Tart. Many of our best puddings are simple and straightforward which I think is one of their strengths. For example, Summer Pudding is made from bread, sugar and soft fruit, but its taste is superb.

It has been a painful task to select traditional pudding recipes from the many available. I just hope that I have included some of your favourites and perhaps brought back happy memories.

Note:
The recipes marked with * are, in my opinion, unsuitable for freezing.

BAKED PUDDINGS

The discovery of the pudding cloth in the seventeenth century was a vital factor in the great expansion of pudding eating, but Elizabethan cooks had already devised another method of cooking puddings avoiding boiling in animal guts. The pudding mixture was baked in a 'coffyn' or 'platter' in the bread or side oven with a pastry crust over it like a tart. In the early part of the seventeenth century, a pudding baked in a pot was still known as a 'pudding pye'. Occasionally, the baking dish was lined with a thin sheet of pastry before the pudding mixture went into it. This practice was more frequent in the eighteenth century. Sometimes the pastry was simply used to garnish the brim of the baking dish, to make it look elegant enough to be brought straight from the oven to the table.

Soon, recipes for baked puddings were appearing regularly in cookery books. They were often based upon rich ingredients and this, together with the fact that an oven had to be heated for their baking, made them puddings for the wealthy rather than the poor. Fresh fruits in season were often substituted for the dried 'plums' in many recipes and baked puddings containing apples, apricots, Seville oranges, lemons and even carrots were common. Specially turned wooden baking dishes were sold in which the puddings could be cooked.

A baked pudding mixture should be slightly softer than for a steamed or boiled pudding to give a crisp surface. If you use water instead of milk to soften the mixture, you will make a lighter pudding. To prevent jam, marmalade or chocolate from caramelising during baking, stand your baking dish in a roasting tin half-filled with water.

Apple and Brandy Humble *(serves 6)*
This is a very interesting version of apple crumble, using wholemeal flour and chopped nuts. It is well worth making a larger quantity of the crumble topping and freezing it. You can use any fruit and try experimenting with different liqueurs and nuts.

2lb (900g) cooking apples
3oz (75g) sultanas or raisins
7oz (200g) soft dark brown sugar
1½ teaspoons (1½ x 5ml)
   ground cinnamon
¼ teaspoon (¼ x 5ml) ground
   cloves

Juice of ½ lemon
1 tablespoon (1 x 15ml) brandy
6oz (175g) wholemeal flour
Pinch of salt
3½oz (90g) butter
1–2oz (25–50g) chopped
   hazelnuts

Peel, core and thinly slice the apples. Add sultanas or raisins, 4oz (125g) sugar, ½ teaspoon (½ x 5ml) cinnamon, ground cloves, lemon juice and brandy. Arrange mixture in a buttered 2pt (1 litre) ovenproof dish.

Sieve together flour, remaining cinnamon and salt into a mixing bowl. Rub 3oz (75g) butter into mixture until it resembles coarse breadcrumbs. Stir in remaining sugar and chopped nuts. Sprinkle over apples and dot with remaining butter. Bake in the centre of a moderate oven (375°F, 190°C; Gas Mark 5) for 45–50 minutes or until apples are tender and crumble topping is crisp and golden brown.

Serve hot with clotted cream, Custard Sauce or Brandy Butter.

My Brother's Apple Brown Betty *(serves 6)*
An original nineteenth-century Brown Betty was made with apples, breadcrumbs and suet and was a popular pudding with the lower-paid country folk. Delicious Brown Betties can be made with many other fruits, but the amount of sugar must be adjusted accordingly. Some of the most successful fruits are rhubarb, plums, gooseberries, damsons, blackcurrants, blackberries and cherries.

3oz (75g) butter
6oz (175g) fresh white
   breadcrumbs
1½lb (675g) cooking apples
4oz (125g) demerara sugar

1 teaspoon (1 x 5ml) ground
   cinnamon
Grated rind and juice of 1 lemon
   or 1 orange
Extra demerara sugar

Melt the butter in a heavy frying pan, add breadcrumbs and cook over moderate heat, stirring continuously to prevent burning, until crumbs are light golden in colour. Peel, core and slice the apples thinly. Mix them with the sugar, cinnamon, grated lemon or orange rind and juice. Butter a 2pt (1 litre) ovenproof dish and put in a thin layer of crumbs, then a layer of apples, then more crumbs, more apples, finishing with a layer of crumbs. Sprinkle with extra demerara sugar and cover with foil. Bake in the centre of a moderate oven (350°F, 180°C; Gas Mark 4) for 20 minutes, then remove foil and bake for a further 35 minutes, or until the top has browned and is crisp, and the apples are soft.

Serve hot with clotted or whipped cream or Custard Sauce.

An Apple and Blackberry Charlotte *(serves 6)*

There is a lovely legend that says this pudding was named after Charlotte, the heroine of Goethe's romance *The Sorrows of Young Werther*, published in 1774.

> Werther had a love for Charlotte
> Such as words could never utter
> Would you know how first he met her?
> She was cutting bread and butter.

In fact, the name for this combination of bread and butter with apple marmalade is probably a corruption of the old English word Charlyt. In old recipes, a 'marmalade' of apples meant apples cooked in butter with sugar and spices until very soft and then beaten to a pulp. Charlottes can be cooked in a special mould or tin — a plain cylinder about 5in (12½cm) deep, with two small ears either side, or in any small cake tin. Don't confuse this pudding with Charlotte Russe which is a cold pudding originating from Russia, using sponge fingers instead of bread and with a cream filling set with gelatine.

There are dozens of versions of Charlotte and almost any fruit is successful, especially rhubarb, pear, blackberry, apricot, plum, damson and gooseberry.

1lb (450g) cooking or firm dessert apples	2–3 tablespoons (2–3 x 15ml) apricot or quince jam
1lb (450g) blackberries	6–8 slices stale white bread
3oz (75g) butter	3–4oz (75–125g) melted butter
Grated rind and juice of 1 lemon	Caster sugar or soft brown sugar for dredging
3oz (75g) caster sugar	
½ level teaspoon (½ x 5ml) ground cinnamon	

Peel, core and slice the apples. Melt 3oz (75g) butter in a heavy pan and add apples and blackberries. Cook over a low heat until soft, stirring from time to time. Add lemon juice, lemon rind, sugar and cinnamon and continue cooking until juices have almost evaporated. Beat until smooth. Sieve apricot or quince jam and stir into apple pulp. Leave to cool.

Butter a charlotte mould or cake tin well. Remove crusts from slices of bread. Trim one slice of bread to fit the bottom of the mould and cut into 6 equal-sized triangles. Cut another slice to fit the top of the mould and again cut into 6 triangles. Cut remaining bread slices into 1½in (3½cm) strips to line the sides of the mould. Dip all pieces of bread in melted butter and arrange strips overlapping each other to line the sides of the mould. Arrange the first 6 buttered triangles to fit the bottom of the mould. Spoon in apple and blackberry mixture, pressing it down well and giving the mould a bang on the table to release any air. Cover with remaining 6 buttered triangles and sprinkle with caster sugar.

Bake in the centre of a fairly hot oven (400°F, 200°C; Gas Mark 6) for 40 minutes. Remove from the oven and press down a little using a plate or spoon. Run a knife round the sides of the mould to loosen it and cover with a serving dish. Invert mould carefully to turn out the charlotte. Dredge with caster or soft brown sugar.

Serve hot with pouring cream, Custard Sauce or Apricot Sauce.

An Apricot Amber Pudding *(serves 6)*
Traditionally, an Amber Pudding was made with apples and baked in a puff-pastry case. It is a very old-fashioned sweet dating back to the 1700s, and can be made with many other fruits such as apples, rhubarb, gooseberries, blackberries, blackcurrants or plums.

6oz (175g) plain flour
2 pinches of salt
1½oz (40g) margarine or butter
1½oz (40g) lard
About 2 tablespoons (2 x 15ml)
   cold water

1lb (450g) fresh apricots
¼pt (150ml) water
8oz (225g) caster sugar
1 teaspoon (1 x 5ml) lemon juice
1oz (25g) unsalted butter
2 eggs, separated

Sieve flour and salt together into a mixing bowl. Cut fats into the flour and rub in using fingertips, until the mixture resembles breadcrumbs. Add enough cold water to mix to a firm dough. Chill for at least 30 minutes.

Wash and stone apricots. Put fruit and water in a heavy saucepan, cover and cook gently until juices run — about 5 minutes. Remove the lid and continue cooking gently until the liquid has evaporated — about 20 minutes. Rub fruit through a sieve. Sweeten with half the sugar and add lemon juice. Stir in the butter. Beat egg yolks and beat into hot apricot pulp. Leave on one side to cool.

Roll out pastry thinly on a lightly floured board and use to line a greased 8in (20cm) shallow ovenproof dish or pie plate. Chill again. Then bake blind for 10 minutes in a fairly hot oven (400°F, 200°C; Gas Mark 6). Remove foil and cook for a further 5 minutes.

Pour cooled apricot mixture into the pastry case and bake for a further 20 minutes. Meanwhile, whisk egg whites with a pinch of salt until stiff, but not dry. Add 2oz (50g) caster sugar and whisk until stiff again. Fold in remaining sugar gently. Reduce oven to 350°F, 180°C; Gas Mark 4). Pile meringue on top of the apricot mixture. Dredge with extra caster sugar and bake in the centre of the oven for 20–30 minutes or until meringue is crisp and lightly browned.

Serve hot or cold with whipped cream and decorate with crystallised apricots and candied angelica.

Apple Cobs *(serves 6)*

Also known as Bomdard'd Apples or Apple Dumplings, and they are as British as steak and kidney pud, although they are also one of the legendary dishes of northern France and several other European countries. The origin of surrounding an apple or any fruit with pastry is very remote but the word dumpling is said to derive from the word dump, one of the meanings of which is a 'thick, solid, shapeless lump'. Dumplings, unfortunately, sometimes answer this description!

The original dumplings were boiled, but in this recipe they are baked. Use a really good quality cooking apple which will go soft and puffy when cooked. You can use shortcrust instead of suet-crust pastry if you want a less rich pud.

12oz (350g) self-raising flour	6 heaped teaspoons (6 x 5ml)
Pinch of salt	mincemeat
6oz (175g) shredded suet	6 cloves
2oz (50g) caster sugar	Water or milk for brushing
About 10 tablespoons	1 egg white
(10 x 15ml) cold water	3 tablespoons (3 x 15ml) clotted
6 medium Bramley apples	cream

Sieve flour and salt together into a mixing bowl. Mix in suet and stir in half the sugar. Add just sufficient water to mix to a soft but not sticky dough. Turn out on to a lightly floured board and divide into 6 equal pieces. Roll out each piece thinly into a square large enough to encase an apple. Peel and core apples and place one in the centre of each pastry square. Fill each apple centre with mincemeat and top with a clove. Brush edge of each pastry square with a little water or milk, draw up corners to meet over the centre of each apple and press edges firmly together. Turn upside-down, and place on a greased baking tray. Decorate with pastry leaves, brush with beaten egg white, and sprinkle with remaining sugar. Bake in the centre of a fairly hot oven (400°F, 200°C; Gas Mark 6) for 30 minutes or until golden brown. Remove from the oven and leave to stand for a few minutes on a warm serving dish. Cut a hole in the top of each dumpling and spoon in some clotted cream, or serve with Custard Sauce or a Hard Sauce.

Variation:
Apple and Blackberry Cobs
Fill apple cavities with blackberries and a little sugar instead of mincemeat. Serve with clotted cream or Brandy and Honey Iced Cream. Try using raspberries in the same way.

Rich Bakewell Pudding *(serves 6)*

This famous Derbyshire pudding has its origins in Elizabethan recipes for a very popular almond pudding where lots of eggs, butter and cream were mixed with pounded almonds and baked 'with paste round the dish' or in a 'coffyn'. There are several 'original' recipes in Derbyshire, and other north-country puddings and pies are clearly of the same family, but generally it is accepted that the pudding was probably first made by a cook at the Rutland Arms in Bakewell two hundred years ago. Jane Austen was reputed to have stayed at this hotel while writing *Pride and Prejudice*.

The original recipe was made in a special oval tin 3in (7½cm) deep and 6in (15cm) wide and had a thick layer of preserved fruit, such as peaches or apricots, and strips of candied citron or orange peel spread over the pastry. A custard made with eggs, butter and sugar and flavoured with what the Bakewellians call 'lemon brandy', brandy flavoured with lemon rind, was poured on top of the preserved fruit and the pudding was baked. Ratafia or almond flavouring is more commonly used now, and flaky or rich shortcrust pastry can be used instead of shortcrust.

6oz (175g) plain flour	3 eggs
Pinch of salt	4oz (125g) caster sugar
1½oz (40g) margarine or butter	4oz (125g) unsalted butter
1½oz (40g) lard	½ teaspoon (½ x 5ml) vanilla or
About 2 tablespoons (2 x 15ml)	ratafia essence
cold water	1 tablespoon (1 x 15ml) brandy
3 heaped tablespoons (3 x 15ml)	4oz (125g) ground almonds
apricot jam	Icing sugar for dredging
1oz (25g) chopped candied peel	

Sieve flour and salt together into a mixing bowl. Rub fats into flour with your fingertips until mixture resembles fine breadcrumbs. Mix with sufficient cold water to make a firm dough. Knead until smooth and roll out on a lightly floured board. Line a greased 8in (20cm) oval pie dish with pastry. Prick the bottom with a fork and spread jam evenly over the pastry. Sprinkle with chopped peel and chill.

Beat eggs and sugar together until pale and thick. Melt the butter and run into egg mixture. Beat together well. Stir in vanilla essence or ratafia and brandy. Fold in ground almonds. Pour mixture over jam and candied peel in the pastry case. Bake in the centre of a fairly hot oven (400°F, 200°C; Gas Mark 6) for 10–15 minutes. Reduce oven temperature to 350°F, (180°C; Gas Mark 4) and bake for a further 20–25 minutes or until filling is set and golden brown. Dredge with sieved icing sugar and serve hot, warm or cold with pouring cream.

Variation:
Alderman's Pudding
A popular pudding in the south of England using apricot jam, but no candied peel or brandy.

A Bedfordshire Clanger *(serves 6)*

Traditionally a suet roly-poly pudding with meat at one end and fruit or jam at the other. It was originally devised for the straw-hat makers of Luton to provide a complete meal while they were away at work, as was the Cornish pasty for the tin miners of Cornwall. This recipe only contains fruit. Any fruit or combination of fruits can be used.

8oz (225g) plain flour	1lb (450g) cooking apples
Pinch of salt	6oz (175g) blackberries
4oz (125g) shredded suet	3oz (75g) caster sugar
6–8 tablespoons (6–8 x 15ml) cold water	Milk and sugar for glazing

Sieve flour and salt together into a mixing bowl. Stir in suet. Add sufficient cold water to mix to a soft, but not sticky, dough, using a palette knife. Gather into a ball and turn out on to a lightly floured board. Knead lightly until smooth. Roll out about ¼in (6mm) thick into a rectangle about 10in x 8in (25cm x 20cm). Peel, core and slice apples. Place apple slices and blackberries on the pastry, sprinkle with sugar and roll up like a Swiss roll. Dampen edges with milk and press firmly together to seal. Turn roly-poly upside-down on a greased baking tray and cut 4 slits across the top to allow steam to escape. Glaze lightly with milk and sugar and bake in a fairly hot oven (400°F, 200°C; Gas Mark 6) for 30–40 minutes or until pastry is golden brown. Serve hot with whipped cream or Custard Sauce and sprinkle with extra sugar.

Burton Joyce *(serves 6)*
The recipe for this pudding was given to me by a friend in our village, whose husband frequently enjoyed it when he was a child. Its origin is somewhat of a mystery although we have found out that there is a village in Nottinghamshire called Burton Joyce.

8oz (225g) self-raising flour	2 eggs
Pinch of salt	2–3 tablespoons (2–3 x 15ml)
3oz (75g) caster sugar	milk
4oz (125g) shredded suet or grated margarine	

Butter a 1½pt (750ml) ovenproof dish well. Sieve flour and salt into a mixing bowl. Stir in sugar and suet or grated margarine. Beat eggs and stir into dry ingredients. Add sufficient milk to mix to a dropping consistency. Turn into the buttered ovenproof dish and bake near the top of a moderate oven (350°F, 180°C; Gas Mark 4) for 35–40 minutes or until well risen and golden brown. Serve hot with hot Jam Sauce poured over the top of the pudding.

Old-fashioned Bread Pud *(serves 6)*
In Plymouth, this very old pudding is called Nelson's Cake after the great man who was obviously a lover of it, because it is also particularly popular in East Anglia, where Nelson was born. The original recipe would have been boiled, but it is now more popular baked. Individual bread puddings were popular in Georgian times — they were baked in buttered teacups.

8oz (225g) stale white bread, with crusts removed	2oz (50g) shredded suet
½pt (250ml) milk	2oz (50g) soft brown sugar
2 tablespoons (2 x 15ml) brandy	2 level teaspoons (2 x 5ml) mixed spice
4oz (125g) dried fruit	1 egg
2oz (50g) chopped candied peel	Grated nutmeg
Grated rind of 1 lemon	Caster sugar for dredging

Butter a 1½pt (750ml) ovenproof dish well. Break the crustless bread into small pieces and put in a mixing bowl. Pour milk and brandy over and leave to soak for at least 30 minutes. Beat out any lumps with a fork. Add fruit, peel, lemon rind, suet, sugar and spice and mix well. Beat egg and stir into mixture to give a soft dropping consistency. Turn into buttered dish, grate a little nutmeg over the top and bake in the centre of a moderate oven (350°F, 180°C; Gas Mark 4) for 1½–2 hours, or until nicely brown on top.

Serve hot or cold, cut in slices and dredged generously with caster sugar and with very cold Brandy Butter, or hot Custard, Lemon, or Orange and Lemon Sauce.

Variation:
Old-fashioned Iced Bread Pud
Make as before, but cook for only 1½ hours. Whisk 2 egg whites with a pinch of salt until very stiff. Whisk in 2oz (50g) caster sugar and then gently fold in another 2oz (50g) caster sugar. Pile meringue on top of bread pudding and replace in the oven for a further 20–30 minutes, or until meringue is crisp and lightly browned.

Gingerbread and Pear Upside-down Pudding *(serves 6)*

This was a popular pudding in Victorian days and looks very pretty. You can bake it in a round or square tin and pipe with whipped cream for a special occasion.

2oz (50g) butter
5oz (150g) soft brown sugar
3 firm pears
6 glacé cherries
6 walnut halves
4oz (125g) margarine or lard
4oz (125g) black treacle
4oz (125g) golden syrup
8oz (225g) plain flour
¼ teaspoon (¼ x 5ml) salt
Pinch of ground cloves

2 teaspoons (2 x 5ml) ground cinnamon
2 teaspoons (2 x 5ml) ground ginger
¼ teaspoon (¼ x 5ml) grated nutmeg
1 level teaspoon (1 x 5ml) bicarbonate of soda
¼ pint (150ml) warm milk
2 eggs

Line the bottom and sides of an 8in (20cm) round cake tin with buttered greaseproof paper. Melt the butter in a saucepan over gentle heat, add 3oz (75g) brown sugar and stir for a few minutes until dissolved. Pour into the bottom of the tin. Peel, halve, and core pears and put a glacé cherry in the centre of each pear half. Arrange pears in a circle cut side down on the butter and sugar mixture with stalk ends facing the centre of the tin. Place walnut halves, cut side down, between the pears.

Put margarine or lard, black treacle, golden syrup and remaining brown sugar in a saucepan and melt over a low heat. Sieve flour, salt and spices together into a mixing bowl. Dissolve soda in warmed milk. Beat eggs and add to milk mixture when it has cooled a little. Make a well in the centre of the dry ingredients and pour in melted treacle mixture, followed by egg mixture. Stir together and beat thoroughly until a smooth batter is formed. Pour carefully over pears and walnuts. Bake in the centre of a moderate oven (350°F, 180°C; Gas Mark 4) for 40–50 minutes or until well risen and firm. (Test with a skewer; it should come out clean.) Remove from the oven and allow to shrink a little before turning out on to a warmed serving plate. Peel off greaseproof paper.

Serve warm with whipped cream or Custard Sauce.

Bread and Butter Pudding *(serves 6–8)* *

This pudding dates back to medieval days, but was especially popular in Victorian times to use up the left-over bread and butter, which appeared daily on every tea-table. This particular recipe is based on one by the nineteenth-century cookery writer Eliza Acton, and by using fruit loaf instead of ordinary bread you get a lighter and fruitier pudding. In Georgian times bread and butter pudding was baked with a 'paste round the edge of the dish' but this practice died out, and the pudding really is filling enough without it. Try baking in individual dishes for a dinner party.

2oz (50g) raisins or sultanas	Grated rind of 1 orange
2 tablespoons (2 x 15ml) rum or brandy	1oz (25g) caster or brown sugar
	³⁄₄pt (400ml) single cream
4–6 slices of fruit loaf	3 eggs
1oz (25g) chopped candied peel	Grated nutmeg
Grated rind of 1 lemon	Caster sugar for sprinkling

Put raisins or sultanas in rum or brandy and leave to soak overnight. (Prepare pudding several hours before you want to cook it to allow bread to soak up some of the cream and eggs.) Butter a 2pt (1 litre) ovenproof dish well. Cut liberally buttered bread into triangles to fit the dish. Drain raisins or sultanas, reserving brandy or rum. Fill buttered dish with alternate layers of buttered bread, raisins or sultanas, chopped peel, and lemon and orange rind, finishing with bread.

Heat sugar and cream slowly until just reaching boiling point. Leave to cool a little. Beat eggs and pour hot cream gradually on to egg mixture, beating continuously. Add reserved rum or brandy and pour over waiting bread. Leave to stand for as long as possible, but at least 2 hours.

Sprinkle the top of the pudding liberally with caster sugar and grated nutmeg. Stand dish in a roasting tin half-filled with water, and bake in the centre of a moderate oven (375°F, 190°C; Gas Mark 5) for 35–40 minutes or until top of pudding is crisp and golden.

Serve warm with clotted cream, Custard Sauce or a Hard Sauce.

Variations:
Bread, Butter and Apricot Pudding *
Add 4oz (125g) dried apricots, soaked overnight, to the layers of raisins or sultanas and chopped peel. Add 1oz (25g) extra white or brown sugar.

Osborne Pudding
Use slices of brown bread instead of fruit loaf, liberally spread with butter and jam, marmalade or mincemeat. Proceed as before. Serve sprinkled with brown sugar.

A Rich Chocolate Pudding *(serves 6–8)*

A very rich and delicious pudding for chocolate lovers, suitable for the most elegant dinner parties. It has a sponge topping with a fudgy chocolate sauce underneath.

4oz (125g) butter
4oz (125g) caster or soft brown
  sugar
2 eggs
½ teaspoon (½ x 5ml) vanilla
  essence
4oz (125g) self-raising flour
1oz (25g) cocoa
1½ teaspoons (1½ x 5ml)
  instant coffee

1–2 tablespoons (1–2 x 15ml)
  warm water
2oz (50g) chopped walnuts

For the Chocolate Sauce:
4oz (125g) brown sugar
1 level tablespoon (1 x 15ml)
  cocoa
¼pt (150ml) hot water
Walnut halves for decorating

Butter a 1½pt (750ml) ovenproof dish well. Cream butter and sugar together until pale and fluffy. Gradually beat in eggs and vanilla essence. Sieve together flour, cocoa and coffee. Fold into creamed mixture and add enough warm water to mix to a soft dropping consistency. Spoon mixture into prepared dish. Sprinkle with chopped walnuts if desired.

To make the sauce, mix together cocoa and brown sugar. Stir in hot water. Pour over the top of the pudding and place the dish in a roasting tin half-filled with water. Bake in the centre of a moderate oven (350°F, 180°C; Gas Mark 4) for 45–60 minutes or until well risen and set. (Test with a skewer, which should come out clean.) Decorate with walnut halves and dredge with sieved icing sugar. Serve warm or cold with whipped cream or a home-made Iced Cream.

Damson Cobbler *(serves 6)*

This pudding presumably takes its name from the scone topping, which does look rather like cobblestones. You can either cut out dough into circles and place them round the edges of the dish, over-lapping each other, or you can lay the dough over like a pie crust and cut it into squares — either way, it is a delicious and economical pudding. Many fruits can be used instead of damsons — plums, greengages, blackcurrants, blackberries, apples, rhubarb, bilberries and gooseberries. This particular recipe is made in Cumbria from local damsons.

2lb (900g) damsons
9oz (250g) caster sugar
¼pt (150ml) water
8oz (225g) self-raising flour
Pinch of salt

2oz (50g) butter or margarine
1 egg
1–2 tablespoons (1–2 x 15ml)
  milk
Granulated sugar for sprinkling

Wash damsons and cook slowly in a heavy saucepan with 8oz (225g) sugar and water until just tender. Remove stones and turn into a buttered ovenproof dish. Leave to cool.

Sieve flour and salt together into a mixing bowl. Stir in remaining sugar and rub in fat. Beat egg and add to mixture with enough milk to make a soft dough. Roll out on a lightly floured board to about ½in (1cm) thick. Cut out dough into rounds with a 2in (5cm) cutter and arrange in a ring around the edge of the dish of fruit with the rounds overlapping each other. Brush scone topping with a little milk, and bake near the top of a hot oven (425°F, 220°C; Gas Mark 7) for 10 minutes. Reduce oven temperature to 375°F, (190°C; Gas Mark 5). Sprinkle the top generously with granulated sugar and bake for a further 5–10 minutes until well risen and golden brown.

Hollygog Pudding *(serves 6)* *
This is a golden syrupy roly-poly which is baked in milk. It was first made in the Oxfordshire village of Kiddington, where it has been passed down among farming families.

8oz (225g) plain flour	4 tablespoons (4 x 15ml) warm
Pinch of salt	golden syrup
4oz (125g) butter or lard	About ½pt (250ml) milk
About 3 tablespoons (3 x 15ml)	
cold water	

Sieve flour and salt into a mixing bowl and rub fat into flour until mixture resembles breadcrumbs. Add water to form a stiff dough. Roll out into a rectangular strip, spread with syrup and roll up like a Swiss roll. Put in a well-buttered oval ovenproof dish and pour over enough milk to come halfway up the side of the pudding. Bake in a fairly hot oven (400°F, 200°C; Gas Mark 6) for 30–45 minutes.

Serve hot in slices with cream or Custard Sauce.

Roly-poly Pudding *(serves 6)*
Also known as Baked Jam Roll or Rolled Jam Pudding, this popular pudding used to be boiled in a cloth or shirt-sleeve, but baking gives the pastry a lovely crisp crust which is usually more popular with children. Mincemeat or golden syrup can be used instead of jam.

8oz (225g) self-raising flour	4 tablespoons (4 x 15ml) warmed
1 teaspoon (1 x 5ml) mixed spice	jam
(optional)	Milk, for brushing
Pinch of salt	1 beaten egg, to glaze
4oz (125g) shredded suet	Caster sugar for sprinkling
6–8 tablespoons (6–8 x 15ml)	1oz (25g) flaked almonds
water	(optional)

Sieve flour, spice, if using, and salt together into a mixing bowl. Stir in suet and add just enough water to mix to a soft, but not sticky, dough. Turn out on to a lightly floured board and roll into a rectangle about 8in x 12in (20cm x 30cm). Spread evenly with warm jam leaving a ½in (1cm) border all the way round. Fold this border over the jam and brush with milk. Roll up fairly loosely and press edges of dough together to seal them. Turn roly-poly upside-down on a greased baking sheet. Brush with beaten egg and sprinkle with caster sugar and flaked almonds if you are using them. Bake in the centre of a fairly hot oven (400°F, 200°C; Gas Mark 6) for 35–40 minutes or until golden brown. Sprinkle with more sugar and serve hot with cream, Custard Sauce or Jam Sauce.

Mother Eve's Pudding *(serves 6)*

Traditionally made with tempting apples under a sponge topping, hence the name! However, you can use any fruit and the flavourings can be varied accordingly by adding spices or orange rind. The Georgian recipe for this pudding was made with suet and included currants as well as the apples. It was also boiled rather than baked.

1½lb (675g) cooking apples	2 eggs
4oz (125g) demerara or caster sugar	¼ teaspoon (¼ x 5ml) vanilla essence
Grated rind of 1 lemon	4oz (125g) self-raising flour
2 cloves	1 tablespoon (1 x 15ml) warm water
1 tablespoon (1 x 15ml) water	Caster sugar for dredging
4oz (125g) unsalted butter	
4oz (125g) caster sugar	

Butter a 2pt (1 litre) ovenproof dish. Peel, core and slice apples thinly and place in a heavy saucepan with sugar, lemon rind, cloves, and 1 tablespoon (1 x 15ml) water. Heat over gentle heat for a few minutes until just tender. Turn into prepared dish and leave to cool.

Cream butter and sugar together in a mixing bowl until pale and fluffy. Beat eggs and add gradually to creamed mixture beating well after each addition. Beat in the vanilla essence, and gently fold sieved flour into creamed mixture. Stir in warm water to make a soft dropping consistency and spread evenly over apples.

Bake in the centre of a moderate oven (375°F, 190°C; Gas Mark 5) for about 1 hour, or until well risen and golden brown (test with a fine skewer which should come out clean). Serve hot or cold, dredged with caster sugar and with cream, Madeira, Custard or Lemon sauce.

Variation:
Apple and Almond Pudding
Substitute 4oz (125g) ground almonds for self-raising flour and continue as before. Serve hot or cold with pouring cream.

A Cherry Batter *(serves 6)* *

This famous pudding from Kent has been eaten at cherry feasts and fairs since the thirteenth century, but probably the idea of combining cherries with batter came over with the Normans and this is a reminder that Kent was one of the first counties to be colonised by the invaders. A very similar dish called *Clafoutis* is still made in some regions of France.

Kent's famous juicy black morello cherries, said to be the best black cherries in the world, should be used to make this delicious pud, but drained tinned black cherries can be used out of season. Traditionally the pudding is served cold, but I prefer it warm.

2oz (50g) plain flour
Pinch of salt
2oz (50g) caster sugar
2 eggs
½pt (250ml) single cream or milk

1 tablespoon (1 x 15ml) cherry brandy or a few drops of vanilla essence
1oz (25g) melted butter
1lb (450g) ripe black cherries
Icing sugar for dredging

Sieve flour and salt together into a bowl. Stir in the caster sugar. Beat eggs and blend gradually into flour mixture. Warm the cream or milk and add slowly to the flour mixture beating vigorously to make a smooth light batter. Stir in cherry brandy or vanilla essence and whisk in melted butter. Put aside to rest while you stone the cherries.

Generously butter a shallow 1pt (500ml) ovenproof porcelain dish or an 8in (20cm) flan tin. Spread prepared cherries over the bottom of the dish or tin and carefully pour over the batter. Dot with a few tiny pieces of butter and bake in the centre of a fairly hot oven (400°F, 200°C; Gas Mark 6) for 20 minutes and then reduce temperature to 375°F (190°C; Gas Mark 5) and cook for a further 20 minutes or until batter is well risen and golden, but still creamy inside. Serve warm, generously dredged with sieved icing sugar and with whipped cream or Custard Sauce. If you want to serve the pudding cold, remove from the dish or tin and serve with pouring or whipped cream.

Nottingham Pudding *(serves 4–6)* *

Also known as Apple-in-and-out, this pudding is a combination of apple and batter, dating back to medieval days when dried fruits, spices and candied peel were put in a batter pudding and served with joints of meat. This tradition has continued in the north of England, where any left-overs are served after the meal with melted butter and treacle, lemon juice and sugar or warmed honey and cinnamon.

4oz (125g) plain flour	1½oz (40g) butter
Pinch of salt	Grated rind of ½ lemon
1 large egg	½ teaspoon (½ x 5ml) ground
¼pt (150ml) milk	cinnamon
¼pt (150ml) water	3oz (75g) soft brown sugar
1lb (450g) cooking apples	1½oz (40g) lard

Sieve flour and salt together into a basin and make a well in the centre. Break the egg into the well and stir to mix with the flour. Gradually add half the milk and water, beating well with a wooden spoon until batter is smooth and creamy. Add remaining liquid, beating with a rotary or electric whisk to keep batter smooth and light. Leave to stand in a cool place for about 30 minutes.

Peel, core and slice the apples. Melt the butter in a heavy frying pan, add apples, lemon rind, cinnamon and sugar, cover and cook gently until apples are just tender.

Put lard in a 7½in (19cm) square baking tin and heat near the top of a hot oven (425°F, 220°C; Gas Mark 7) until the fat is smoking. Remove from the oven and carefully add apple mixture and pour batter over. Return to the oven for about 20 minutes and then reduce temperature to 375°F (190°C; Gas Mark 5) for a further 20–25 minutes or until batter is firm and golden brown. (This batter pudding will not rise as much as a Yorkshire pudding, because of the fruit.)

Variation:
Sweet Batter Pudding

Leave out the apples and bake a plain batter. Serve immediately with melted golden syrup or honey poured over the pudding, and sprinkled with caster sugar, or serve with Syrup, Jam or Marmalade Sauce. You can vary this recipe by adding 2oz (50g) raisins or sultanas.

Tewkesbury Saucer Batters *(serves 4 or 8)* *

Saucers were used for baking small savoury and sweet pies and puddings years before they were used under teacups, and a few recipes still survive. This one comes from Gloucestershire and is for batter puddings baked in saucers. You can serve them filled with fresh soft fruit such as raspberries, blackberries, loganberries or strawberries. They make a very unusual pudding for a dinner party. The quantities given here will make 4 saucer batters which should be enough for 8 people, but if your guests or family have large appetites and can polish off a saucer batter each, you will have to make more batter!

8oz (225g) plain flour	1pt (500ml) milk
¼ teaspoon (¼ x 5ml) salt	1½lb (675g) soft fruit
2 eggs, separated	4–6oz (125–175g) sugar

Sieve flour and salt together into a mixing bowl. Make a well in the centre and put in egg yolks. Beat in egg yolks gradually, adding milk a little at a time and beating continuously until the mixture becomes a smooth creamy batter. Leave in a cool place for at least 30 minutes, for the starch to begin to break down.

Meanwhile, well butter 4 *ovenproof* saucers. Put the fruit in an oven-proof dish, sprinkle with sugar, cover and put in the oven while it is heating up until the juices begin to run. Taste to see if sweet enough. (Be careful not to cook strawberries more than a few seconds or they will go mushy.) Take the fruit from the oven and leave on one side.

Whisk egg whites until very stiff, and fold into batter. Divide batter between 4 prepared saucers, and put in the top of a hot oven (450°F, 230°C; Gas Mark 8). Bake for about 15–20 minutes or until golden brown and coming away from the edges of the saucers. Remove from the oven when cooked, and slide on to a warmed serving dish. Sprinkle with caster sugar and fill each batter with fruit.

Serve hot with whipped cream.

Raspberry Crumble *(serves 6)*
In this recipe fresh raspberries are used, but many other fruits are suitable and you can enjoy yourself experimenting both with fruits and flavourings in the crumble topping and the fruit base, e.g. plum and cinnamon, rhubarb and orange, blackcurrants and mint, goose-berry and orange, rhubarb and ginger.

2lb (900g) fresh raspberries	3oz (75g) butter
7oz (200g) caster sugar	2oz (50g) chopped walnuts
6oz (175g) plain flour	(optional)
Pinch of salt	

Place raspberries and 4oz (125g) sugar in a buttered 2pt (1 litre) oven-proof dish. Sieve flour and salt together. Rub butter into flour until it resembles coarse breadcrumbs and stir in 3oz (75g) sugar and chop-ped nuts. Sprinkle over top of raspberries and bake in the centre of a fairly hot oven (400°F, 200°C; Gas Mark 6) for about 45 minutes or until top is crisp and golden. Serve hot with clotted or pouring cream or Custard Sauce.

An Excellent Lemon Pudding *(serves 4–6)*

This lovely pudding is based on a very old recipe which was baked in a dish lined with puff pastry. By whisking egg whites and adding just before baking, the pudding will be very light. You may need to cover with greaseproof paper if the top is getting too brown too quickly before the underneath has set. This pudding separates out during cooking into a tangy custard layer with a featherlight sponge topping. An orange pudding can be made in the same way using 2 oranges.

2oz (50g) butter	2 eggs, separated
4oz (125g) caster sugar	8 fl oz (225ml) milk
Grated rind and juice of 1 lemon	2oz (50g) plain flour

Cream butter and sugar together with lemon rind. Beat egg yolks into creamed mixture very gradually. When the mixture is very light, beat in lemon juice and milk. Fold in sieved flour. Whisk egg whites until stiff and fold into lemon mixture.

Pour pudding into well-buttered 2pt (1 litre) ovenproof dish and stand in a roasting tin half-filled with warm water. Bake in the centre of a moderate oven (375°F, 190°C; Gas Mark 5) for 40–45 minutes or until sponge topping is golden brown and firm. Serve hot with pouring cream, or a home-made Iced Cream; or cold, decorated with whipped cream and fresh lemon slices.

Baked Pear and Brandy Dumplings *(serves 6)* *

These delicious crisp pear dumplings are served with brandy- or rum-flavoured whipped cream and are lovely for a dinner party. Peaches or apples can also be used.

1½lb (675g) shortcrust pastry	3oz (75g) icing sugar
6 large firm dessert pears	1 beaten egg
Juice of 1 lemon	Extra icing sugar for dredging

Peel and core pears carefully, keeping them whole. Brush all over with lemon juice to prevent them going brown. Roll in icing sugar.

Roll out pastry on a lightly floured board and cut out 6 circles using a 6in or 7in (15cm or 17½cm) tea-plate. Place a pear in the centre of each circle, brush edges of pastry with beaten egg and bring up around each pear, pinching edges at the stalk end. Place pastry-wrapped pears on a greased baking tray and glaze with beaten egg. Using pastry trimmings, cut out some leaves and decorate tops of pear dumplings, glazing again with beaten egg. Bake near the top of a moderate oven (375°F, 190°C; Gas Mark 5) for 35–40 minutes or until pastry is golden brown and the pears are soft.

Serve hot or cold, dredged with icing sugar and with whipped cream, sweetened and flavoured with brandy or rum and a pinch of ground cinnamon or ginger.

CREAMS, FLUMMERIES, FOOLS, SNOWS AND SYLLABUBS

England's elaborate and elegant cold sweets were famous throughout Europe in Tudor times. The sweet course at a great feast was then known as the 'banquet' and consisted of preserved fruits, creams, flummeries, jellies, fools and tarts. Some noblemen built banqueting houses in their grounds to serve the banquet privately to their guests after the main part of the meal had been eaten in the Great Hall. On prosperous farms these dishes were less elaborately served and decorated, but the same cold sweets, rich with cream, butter, eggs and fruit, were made for special occasions.

The ancestor of creams, fools and flummeries was the medieval meatless pottage known as 'frumenty' made from breadcrumbs, oats, rice, wheat or barley, stewed in almond milk and served on fasting days. Cream later replaced the milk and almonds were used for thickening. This dish was known as 'whitepot'. By the seventeenth century, the almonds were often omitted and the cream was thickened with eggs. Sometimes fresh or boiled cream was sweetened and mixed with fruit pulp to make fruit fools or creams.

In the eighteenth century, gooseberries and orange juice combined with eggs were made into fools and recipes for almond and codlin or apple cream were very common. These fruit creams were served in the second course alongside flummeries and jellies. Iced creams and snows were also being made at this time.

The syllabub of Tudor and Stuart times was designed to be drunk and consisted of white wine, cider or fruit juice, sugar and nutmeg to which cream or milk was added with considerable force — usually directly from the cow. The object was to produce a frothy head to the drink with a clear liquid below. The latter was drunk from the spout of a 'syllabub pot', while the creamy foam was eaten. In Georgian times the cream and wine were whisked together with lemon juice, and these whipped-cream syllabubs remained a very popular dessert all through the eighteenth century, and indeed have become fashionable again in the last few years.

There are so many delicious recipes for these creamy puddings that it has been impossible to include even a reasonable number in this chapter, but I hope you will enjoy those I have mentioned and that they will inspire you to experiment yourselves.

Atholl Brose *(serves 6)* *

This is really a hot Scottish drink similar to the Elizabethan version of syllabub, but in some areas of Scotland it is thickened with toasted oatmeal, as in this recipe, and served as a pudding. Fragrant heather honey should be used if possible, and purists also say that the clear pure Scotch whisky gives the best result.

2oz (50g) coarse oatmeal	Scotch whisky
2oz (50g) clear heather honey	2 teaspoons (2 x 5ml) lemon juice
3 tablespoons (3 x 15ml)	¾pt (400ml) double cream

Toast oatmeal for a few minutes under a hot grill shaking frequently until it becomes an even light brown. Leave to cool. Warm the honey until it melts, remove from heat and blend in whisky and lemon juice. Whisk cream until it begins to thicken. Stir in warmed honey and whisky mixture. Continue to whisk until mixture stands in peaks. Fold in oatmeal. Pour into one glass dish or individual glasses and chill. Serve chilled with fresh soft fruit.

Victorian Apple Snow *(serves 6)* *

This dish of apples and whisked egg whites has very ancient ancestors. Egg whites were first beaten in Elizabethan days and used to produce their 'dishful of snow', a spectacular centrepiece for the banquet course following a festal meal. They were beaten with thick cream, rose-water and sugar until the froth rose and was gathered in a colander. This was built up over an apple and a thick bush of rosemary on a platter. In some versions the 'snow' was gilded as a final touch.

The same dish with the addition of whipped cream continued into the eighteenth century as Snow Cream or Blanched Cream. Another form with the addition of apple pulp came to be known as Apple Snow and other seasonal fruit pulps were also used. In Victorian times the cream was omitted and became the pudding that we know today.

2lb (900g) Bramley apples	Grated rind of 1 lemon
1 tablespoon (1 x 15ml) lemon juice	4–6oz (125–175g) caster sugar
	4 egg whites
3 tablespoons (3 x 15ml) cold water	¼pt (150ml) whipping cream for decoration

Peel, core and slice apples. Put in a heavy saucepan with lemon juice, water, and lemon rind. Cover and cook over very low heat, stirring occasionally until very tender and fluffy, about 20 minutes. Remove from heat and beat until smooth with a wooden spoon. Add sugar to taste. Set aside and leave to cool.

Whisk egg whites until very stiff. Lightly fold into cold apple pulp. Pile into a pretty glass dish or individual glasses, and refrigerate. Just before serving, decorate with whipped cream and crystallised flowers or fresh flowers — daisies look lovely with this simple pudding. Serve with Cigarette Biscuits, Cats' Tongues or Sponge Fingers.

Damson Snow *(serves 6)*
This can be frozen and served as an iced cream.

2lb (900g) damsons	2 tablespoons (2 x 15ml) brandy
6oz (175g) caster sugar	or Marsala
1/4pt (150ml) cold water	3 egg whites
3/4pt (400ml) double cream	

Put washed and destalked damsons into a saucepan with sugar and water. Bring slowly to the boil and cook gently for 10–15 minutes or until fruit is tender. Rub through a sieve and leave damson pulp to get cold.

Lightly whip cream with brandy or Marsala until thick. Whisk egg whites until stiff and fold into cream mixture. Stir in damson pulp reserving 2 tablespoons (2 x 15ml) for decoration. Pour into individual glasses and chill well. Put glasses on doyley-covered saucers, decorated with a few fresh flowers or leaves. Just before serving, stir in reserved damson pulp to give a marbled effect, or just top with damson pulp. Serve with any home-made biscuits.

Variation:
Edinburgh fog
Omit damson pulp and replace brandy with sweet sherry. Sweeten with 2oz (50g) caster sugar and stir in 2oz (50g) ratafias. Serve well chilled with a bowl of fresh raspberries or strawberries and sprinkled with toasted flaked almonds.

Codlin Cream *(serves 6)*
Codlin is the old English name for an apple, coming from the old verb to coddle or to stew. Apple pulp is flavoured with rum and folded into whipped cream. Many other fruits can be used in place of the apples, but you will have to adjust the sugar and cooking time accordingly.

2lb (900g) Bramley cooking apples	4–6oz (125–175g) soft brown sugar
3 tablespoons (3 x 15ml) cold water	2oz (50g) raisins
2 cloves	2 tablespoons (2 x 15ml) dark rum
1oz (25g) butter	1/2pt (250ml) double cream
1/2 teaspoon (1/2 x 5ml) ground cinnamon	

Peel, core and slice apples. Put in saucepan with water, cloves, butter and cinnamon. Cover and cook gently for about 20 minutes or until very tender. Beat to a pulp and sweeten with sugar to taste. Leave to cool. Heat raisins gently in rum until plump, stir into apple pulp and leave to go completely cold.

Whip cream lightly and fold into apple mixture. Taste to see if more sugar is needed. Pile into pretty individual glasses and serve chilled, with Sponge Fingers or Brandy Snaps. Decorate with fresh flowers.

Gooseberry and Elderflower Fool *(serves 8–10)*

Gooseberry fool has been very popular for centuries, but was particularly loved by the Victorians, who made it with egg-thickened custard and cream. Indeed, the gooseberry was the Victorians' favourite fruit, especially in the north of England, where it is still grown far more than in the south. In this recipe, the fool is flavoured with elderflowers which give it a delicate grapy taste. Elderflowers were used widely in the past to flavour jellies, creams and flummeries, particularly those made with gooseberries. Pick the elderflowers in June and early July when in full bloom (the same time as gooseberries are ripe), preferably on a dry day. They can be dried and stored successfully to use out of season.

This fool can be frozen and served as an iced cream.

2lb (900g) green gooseberries	2 elderflower heads
3 tablespoons (3 x 15ml) cold water	1pt (500ml) double cream
8oz (225g) caster sugar	¼pt (150ml) single cream

Wash and top and tail gooseberries. Put in a heavy saucepan with water and sugar. Tie elderflowers in a piece of clean muslin and add to the saucepan. Heat the fruit gently to the boil and simmer for about 20 minutes or until the fruit is very soft. Remove elderflowers and rub gooseberries through a sieve. Taste and add more sugar if necessary and leave to cool completely.

Whip double cream until thick and just beginning to hold its shape. Fold into gooseberry purée and pile into individual glasses or custard pots. Chill well.

Serve with a thin layer of single cream on top of gooseberry fool and decorate with pink rosebuds or crystallised rose petals. Accompany with Cats' Tongues or Sponge Fingers.

Blackcurrant and Mint Fool *(serves 8–10)*

The British fruit fool, probably named after the French verb *fouler* meaning to crush, is the most delicious and refreshing of British puddings. It consists of nothing more than a smooth sweetened fruit purée, stirred into fresh thick cream. However, the early cookery writers describe much richer fools of roughly crushed gooseberries, raspberries, strawberries, redcurrants, apples, mulberries, apricots and figs thickened with eggs and creams and flavoured with wine and spices, perfumed sugar and lemon peel. At some stage, the eggs and extra flavourings were omitted and the simple fool, as we know it, emerged. Any fruit can be used, but I think berries, currants and apricots the most successful.

This fool can also be frozen and served as an iced cream.

1½lb (675g) blackcurrants
8oz (225g) caster sugar
2 tablespoons (2 x 15ml) lemon juice
1pt (500ml) double cream

1 tablespoon (1 x 15ml) chopped fresh mint
2 tablespoons (2 x 15ml) crème de cassis

Wash and top and tail blackcurrants. Put in heavy saucepan with sugar, lemon juice and mint. Cook over a gentle heat, stirring well, until soft and any liquid has evaporated. Rub through a sieve and leave to get completely cold. Stir in liqueur. Whip cream until just thick enough to hold its shape and stir in fruit purée. Taste and add more sugar if necessary. Chill before serving.

Serve fool in glasses or custard cups, standing on doyley-covered saucers and decorated with sprigs of crystallised mint leaves or simple fresh flowers. Shortbread Hearts, Sponge Fingers, or Cats' Tongues go very well with fools.

Lemon Solid (serves 4–6)*
This pudding's ancestor was the posset, which was an Elizabethan drink of milk, curdled with sack. A richer posset for the gentry was made with cream and sack, later replaced by sherry or brandy. Instead of being thickened with breadcrumbs like a posset, it was thickened with eggs, Naples biscuit crumbs (an almond-flavoured biscuit), or with beaten (ground) almonds. Lemon Solid is found in varying forms in many old cookery books and is one of the glories of British cooking, despite its rather uninspiring name.

29

1pt (500ml) double cream   5oz (150g) caster sugar
Grated rind and juice of 2 lemons   3–4 macaroons

Put cream, lemon rind and sugar in a saucepan. Stir over gentle heat for about 10 minutes until sugar has completely dissolved, bringing just to the boil. Cool, stirring from time to time and when almost cold add strained lemon juice. Crumble macaroons and put in the bottom of a pretty glass bowl. Pour cold cream mixture over macaroons. Chill overnight in refrigerator.

Serve chilled and decorated with whipped cream and crystallised violets or strips of blanched lemon rind.

Gooseberry Tansy *(serves 4)* *

This very old pudding was so called from the use of a herb called 'tansy'. It was chopped up with the fruit, but is seldom used in cookery today as it has rather a bitter flavour. However, the name continues. Apples, rhubarb or plums can be used instead of gooseberries.

1lb (450g) green gooseberries   2 tablespoons (2 x 15ml) caster
4oz (125g) unsalted butter   sugar
2 egg yolks   Juice of ½ lemon
¼pt (150ml) double cream

Simmer gooseberries in the butter until cooked — about 15 minutes. Remove from heat and cool a little. Stir in beaten egg yolks and lightly whipped cream. Sweeten with sugar to taste. Bring to the boil very gently and when thick, turn into a china serving bowl. Sprinkle with caster sugar and lemon juice. Serve hot or cold with Sponge Fingers.

Fine Orange Flummery *(serves 6)* *

Flummery is a lovely pale slippery pudding related to syllabub and custard, and is a delicious pure white jelly. In medieval days cereals such as rice, oats or sago were cooked long and slowly with milk and flavourings. This was really the beginning of flummery. In Tudor and Stuart times it became a much richer dish of cream flavoured with spices, orange flower water, rose-water, almonds or wine, set with calves' feet or isinglass. It was often coloured and eaten in the second course with cream or wine poured over. For special occasions, it was made in the most elaborate moulds for 'set-piece dishes', such as flummery fish in a pond of jelly, or flummery eggs in a hen's nest of shredded lemon peel set in jelly!

Flummery is now easily set with gelatine and should be made in the prettiest mould you can find. It is still possible to pick up elaborate Victorian china and glass jelly moulds in antique and junk shops fairly cheaply. If possible, this dish should be made the day before you want to serve it.

1pt (500ml) double cream	3 tablespoons (3 x 15ml) warm
2oz (50g) caster sugar	water
Grated rind and juice of	1oz (25g) powdered gelatine
2 oranges	
1 tablespoon (1 x 15ml) orange	
flower water	

Put cream, sugar, orange rind and juice and orange flower water in a heavy saucepan and heat very gently until sugar is completely dissolved and cream is just coming to the boil. Leave on one side to cool.

Put warm water into a cup and sprinkle over gelatine. Stand the cup in a pan of water and heat gently, stirring, until the gelatine has dissolved. Pour gelatine mixture through a warmed sieve into cream mixture. Stir well. Pour into a wetted mould and leave to cool. Refrigerate overnight.

To turn out, dip mould quickly in hot water. Serve chilled with a bowl of soft fruit and whipped cream.

Variations:
A Fine Orange and Madeira Flummery
Replace orange flower water with Madeira or sweet sherry.

An Almond Flummery
Omit orange flower water, orange rind and juice. Replace with 4oz (125g) ground almonds and 4–5 drops almond essence.

Boodles Orange Fool *(serves 4–6)* *
A speciality at Boodles Club, a London club in St James's Street, which was founded in 1763. It sounds simple, but is very delicious. The idea of combining sponge with fruit fool dates back to the eighteenth-century version with ratafias.

4 sponge cakes	2–3oz (50–75g) caster sugar
Grated rind and juice of 1 lemon	1pt (500ml) double cream
Grated rind and juice of	Crystallised orange slices
2 oranges	Crystallised angelica

Cut sponge cakes into ½in (1cm) strips and line the base of a glass serving dish, or individual glass dishes. Mix rind and juice of fruit with sugar and stir until dissolved. Whip half the cream until thick, but not stiff, and beat juice into cream slowly. Taste for sweetness. Spoon over sponge cakes and chill thoroughly for 2 or 3 hours, until juice has soaked into sponge and cream has set. Whip remaining cream stiff, and pipe on top of pudding to decorate. Garnish with crystallised orange slices and angelica.

Serve the pudding on a doyley-covered plate or saucers decorated with fresh ivy, rose or fern leaves.

An Orange (or Lemon) Posset *(serves 6)* *

A posset was an Elizabethan drink made of milk curdled with sack, claret, beer, ale, orange or lemon juice, rather like a syllabub. Breadcrumbs were added to thicken the posset so that it could be eaten rather than drunk. Later, these were omitted and beaten egg whites were used instead to make it lighter and not so rich.

1pt (500ml) double cream
Grated rind of ½ lemon
Grated rind of 1 orange (or lemon)
¼pt (150ml) dry white wine
2 tablespoons (2 x 15ml) orange or lemon juice
2 tablespoons (2 x 15ml) lemon juice

4oz (125g) caster sugar
3 large egg whites
2 tablespoons (2 x 15ml) caster sugar
Orange or lemon rind or segments for decoration

Beat cream and lemon and orange rind in a mixing bowl until thick. Beat in wine until thick again. Add orange and lemon juice very gradually, beating all the time. Add 4oz (125g) caster sugar and beat until stiff. Whisk egg whites until stiff and standing in peaks. Whisk in 2 tablespoons (2 x 15ml) sugar until smooth and glossy. Fold egg whites into cream mixture. Pile into a pretty glass or china bowl. Chill well.

Serve chilled and decorated with orange or lemon rind or segments of orange or lemon and crystallised mint leaves or pistachio nuts. Serve Cats' Tongues or Orange and Almond Crisps with your posset.

A Raspberry Syllabub Trifle *(serves 6–8)* *

A trifle with a syllabub topping instead of cream and custard, which was the very early version of a trifle. Try using strawberries instead of raspberries, and varying flavourings of syllabub topping — which is best started the day before you want to make your trifle.

Finely pared rind of 2 oranges
Juice of 1 orange
2 tablespoons (2 x 15ml) brandy
¼pt (150ml) white wine, dry sherry or Madeira
3oz (75g) caster sugar
8 trifle sponge cakes
8oz (225g) apple or quince jelly

4oz (125g) ratafias
8–12oz (225–350g) fresh or frozen raspberries
½pt (250ml) double cream
Crystallised orange slices and mint leaves
2oz (50g) ratafias for decoration

Put orange rind and orange juice in a bowl with wine and brandy and leave overnight. Next day, strain wine and orange mixture into a saucepan. Add sugar and heat gently until sugar has dissolved. Pour into a large deep bowl and leave to cool.

Split sponge cakes in half and spread liberally with jelly. Put half in the bottom of your prettiest glass or china dish. Sprinkle with half the ratafias, followed by half the raspberries.

Gradually stir cream into the wine and orange mixture, beating until it 'ribbons' and stands in soft peaks. Cover raspberries and sponge with half the syllabub mixture. Put rest of split sponge cakes and ratafias in the trifle dish, followed by the remainder of the raspberries, reserving a few of the best berries for decorating. Cover with remaining syllabub topping and decorate with crystallised orange slices, mint leaves and reserved raspberries rolled in caster sugar and ratafias. Serve chilled. (If you want, make this trifle in several more layers.)

Variation:
Lemon Posset Trifle
Use lemon or orange posset as a topping instead of syllabub.

Rhubarb and Orange Fool *(serves 8–10)*
Rhubarb was one of the latest garden fruits to be cultivated for eating in Britain. It had been grown in China since Roman times for its root, a powerful purgative, which was exported to the west, and in Tudor times the plants themselves were introduced into English herb gardens and *medicinal* rhubarb became a garden crop. The rhubarb we know now first arrived in the seventeenth century when John Parkinson received seeds from Italy which he planted in his garden. Its cultivation spread rapidly throughout Britain and it has remained one of the most popular garden fruits.

This fool is also known as Spring Fool. Try mixing the rhubarb pulp with other fruit pulps like apple, plum, gooseberry and raspberry.

2lb (900g) rhubarb	8oz (225g) caster or soft brown
Grated rind of 1 orange	sugar
½ teaspoon (½ x 5ml) ground	1pt (500ml) double or whipping
ginger	cream
2in (5cm) stick cinnamon	2 tablespoons (2 x 15ml) orange
1oz (25g) unsalted butter	liqueur

Cut the rhubarb in short lengths. Put in a large saucepan with orange rind, ginger, cinnamon stick, butter and sugar. (If you use brown sugar the colour of your fool will be pale brown instead of pink.) Cook over a gentle heat, stirring until soft and leave to simmer until most of the liquid has evaporated and a soft rhubarb pulp is left. Remove cinnamon stick and sieve. Allow to go cold.

Whip the cream with the liqueur until thick enough to hold its shape. Fold in cold rhubarb pulp very lightly to give a marbled effect. Taste, and add more sugar if necessary. Spoon fool into a deep glass bowl or individual glasses, and chill well before serving. Decorate with crystallised primroses or fresh flowers and candied angelica. Serve with Cats' Tongues, Macaroons, or Sponge Fingers.

London Syllabub *(serves 4–6)* *

Syllabub is one of the oldest-known English dishes. In Elizabethan times it was a drink popular at feasts, consisting of a bubbling wine, mixed with frothing milk. The cow was milked straight into the wine or sack mixed with sugar and spices in the syllabub pot, so that the new warm milk fell in a froth. The contents of the pot were left undisturbed for an hour or two, by which time a honeycombed curd had formed on the top, leaving alcoholic whey underneath.

Later, in the seventeenth and eighteenth centuries, syllabub was made with whipped-up cream, rather than milk and white wine, and cider or fruit juice, which was well sweetened with sugar and flavoured with lemon or nutmeg. It became, in fact, the pudding we know today. Allow orange or lemon rind and rosemary to infuse in the spirits overnight if possible.

Finely pared rind of 2 oranges or 1 lemon
Juice of 1 orange or lemon
Sprig of fresh rosemary
¼pt (150ml) white wine, dry sherry or Madeira

2 tablespoons (2 x 15ml) brandy
3oz (75g) caster sugar or honey
½pt (250ml) double cream
Orange or lemon peel or sprigs of rosemary for decoration

Put orange or lemon rind, orange or lemon juice, and rosemary in a bowl with the wine and brandy and leave overnight. Next day, strain wine and orange or lemon mixture into a saucepan. Add sugar or honey and heat gently until sugar has dissolved. Pour into a large deep bowl and leave to cool. Gradually stir in the cream, beating until it 'ribbons' and stands in soft peaks. (Don't use an electric blender or the cream may become grainy.) Pour into your prettiest glasses, or custard cups, and chill. Serve decorated with strips of orange peel or sprigs of rosemary. Accompany with Orange and Almond Crisps or Brandy Snaps, and a few black grapes dipped in beaten egg white and coated with caster sugar.

Variation:
Strawberry Syllabub
Use sweet white or rosé wine and add a pinch of ground mace before infusing with the orange rind. The following day, slice 8–12oz (225–350g) strawberries reserving the best berries for decoration. Put remainder into pretty wine glasses and top with syllabub made as before. Serve decorated with reserved berries and toasted flaked almonds.

Marbled Rose Cream *(serves 8–10)*
This delicate raspberry cream is flavoured with rose-water, which you can buy at most good grocers' and chemists'. It was a favourite flavouring in Tudor and Stuart cookery. The perfuming of food was a custom borrowed from the French where it enjoyed a great vogue through the sixteenth and seventeenth centuries. Rose bushes, specifically for making rose-water, were grown in the kitchen garden alongside fruit bushes. Any soft fruits can be used in this recipe. This can be frozen and served as an iced cream.

2lb (900g) fresh or frozen raspberries
9oz (250g) caster sugar
2 tablespoons (2 x 15ml) cold water

1pt (500ml) double cream
2 tablespoons (2 x 15ml) rose-water or kirsch

Put 1lb (450g) raspberries into a saucepan with 6oz (175g) caster sugar and water. Bring gently to the boil and simmer for a few minutes, or until raspberries start to yield their juice. Push through a sieve and leave to cool. Whip cream until thick and add remaining caster sugar gradually. Mash remaining raspberries, reserving a few of the best berries for decoration. Mix very thoroughly into whipped cream and stir in rose-water or kirsch. Now add cooked raspberry pulp, stirring just enough to give a marbled effect. Pour into your prettiest glass bowl and refrigerate for at least 3 hours before serving. Decorate with reserved berries rolled in a little caster sugar and crystallised mint leaves.

Whim-wham *(serves 6)* *
This Edwardian trifle uses Naples biscuits instead of sponge cake, and syllabub instead of custard. It is delicious, and very rich. Sponge fingers or boudoir biscuits can be used instead of Naples biscuits which were the foundation for many eighteenth- and nineteenth-century desserts.

½pt (250ml) double cream
2oz (50g) caster sugar
2 tablespoons (2 x 15ml) white wine
Grated rind of 1 lemon

6 sponge fingers (see recipe on page 125) or boudoir biscuits
8oz (225g) redcurrant, quince or apple jelly
1oz (25g) chopped candied orange peel

Put cream, sugar, wine, and lemon rind into a large bowl and whisk until thick. Slice sponge finger biscuits and spoon layers of syllabub, biscuits and jelly alternately in a pretty glass bowl, ending with a layer of syllabub. Sprinkle with chopped candied orange peel and chill overnight. Decorate as prettily as you can.

ICED CREAMS

Iced cream became popular in Britain in the eighteenth century as a result of the development of ice houses on country estates. Large quantities of ice were delivered in wagons and stored in specially built houses, brick-lined pits or cellars to help preserve fresh produce like meat and fish. If the winter was cold enough, ice was taken from local ponds and lakes, but if not, it was brought in from the Lake District and Scotland. Later, ice came back in the holds of ships from North America as ballast. The earliest iced creams really were *iced* creams or frozen fruit fools. At first these were prepared in the tin icing pots with close-fitting lids, which were buried in pails full of ice, but later, pewterers started producing sets of basins — an inner smaller one to contain the fruit and an outer larger one to hold ice all around it.

You can still make iced cream by freezing fruit purée and cream but it is rather extravagant. By adding beaten eggs, a less expensive and lighter ice is produced which also softens more quickly for serving. It is great fun experimenting with iced creams and the possible variations seem endless. My favourite basic recipe was given to me by my mother-in-law who was a wonderful cook and a very special friend.

Brown Bread Iced Cream *(serves 6–8)*
This ice cream, using brown breadcrumbs, was introduced later in the eighteenth century than the fruit iced creams but was not popular until late Victorian and Edwardian days when it was served as a country weekend treat. The breadcrumbs can be fried or baked in the oven with the butter and sugar.

3oz (75g) wholemeal bread	4oz (125g) caster sugar
2oz (50g) unsalted butter	2 tablespoons (2 x 15ml) rum,
3oz (75g) caster or soft brown	brandy or Madeira
sugar	¾pt (400ml) double or whipping
4 eggs, separated	cream

Prepare breadcrumbs by frying in butter until crisp and adding the sugar. Let this caramelise, and then cool completely. Crush with a rolling pin. If you want to bake breadcrumbs, spread them out on a baking tray. Add melted butter and sprinkle with sugar. Bake in a moderate oven (350°F, 180°C; Gas Mark 4) for about 30 minutes or until crisp. Cool and then crush.

To prepare basic ice cream, beat egg yolks with sugar and brandy, rum or Madeira. Whip cream until it holds its shape and add to egg mixture. Whisk egg whites until stiff and fold into cream and egg mixture. Freeze in a lidded container for about 1 hour and then stir in prepared breadcrumbs. Freeze again.

Remove from freezer to refrigerator at least 30 minutes before serving. Scoop into pretty glasses. Decorate with crystallised violets, and serve with hot Butterscotch Sauce, or hot Chocolate Sauce and accompanied by Brandy Snaps.

Rich Coffee and Praline Iced Cream *(serves 6–8)*

For praline:
3oz (75g) unblanched
   almonds
3oz (75g) granulated sugar

For ice cream:
4 eggs, separated
4oz (125g) caster sugar
3 tablespoons (3 x 15ml) coffee
   essence
3/4pt (400ml) double cream

To make praline, place unblanched almonds and the granulated sugar in a small, preferably non-stick, frying pan. Heat gently until the sugar melts. Stir with a metal spoon until a rich dark brown. Turn out on to an oiled baking tray and leave to set.

To make ice cream, beat egg yolks with caster sugar and coffee essence. Whip cream and add to egg yolk mixture. Whip egg whites until stiff and gently stir into egg and cream mixture.

Crush set praline into a coarse powder with a rolling pin or in a nut mill or a mincer. Stir this into ice-cream mixture. Freeze in ice trays or any container until half-set; then stir to distribute praline evenly. Return to the freezer until firm.

Remove from the freezer 20 minutes before you want to serve and put in refrigerator. Serve scooped in individual glasses. Decorate with a sprinkling of extra praline powder if you wish.

Variations:
Praline
Omit coffee essence and proceed as above.

Rich Coffee and Walnut
As above, but use 3oz (75g) walnuts instead of almonds and only heat nuts and sugar until *light* brown.

Walnut
Omit coffee essence and use walnuts instead of almonds and soft brown sugar instead of caster if you wish. Serve topped with Butterscotch Sauce or hot Chocolate Sauce.

Chestnut and Chocolate Iced Cream *(serves 6–8)*

Years ago, chestnuts were grown and used in cooking much more than they are now. Indeed, nowadays they seem to be imported from France and only appear at Christmas, so we have to use tinned chestnut purée the rest of the year. However, this does save a lot of work and is available at most good grocers'. You will find this ice cream very delicate and unusual in flavour. For a change, try leaving out the chocolate.

4 eggs, separated
4oz (125g) caster or soft brown
  sugar
2–3 drops vanilla essence
8oz (225g) tin unsweetened
  chestnut purée

¾pt (400ml) double or whipping
  cream
3oz (75g) plain chocolate

Beat egg yolks with sugar and vanilla essence. Stir in chestnut purée. Whip cream until it stands in soft peaks and add to chestnut mixture. Whisk egg whites until stiff and fold gently into mixture. Pour into a lidded container and freeze for about 1½ hours until mushy. Melt plain chocolate and cool.

Remove ice cream from freezer and stir gently. Pour in cooled chocolate and stir. Replace in freezer and leave to freeze completely.

Take ice cream out of freezer 30 minutes before you want to serve it, and leave in refrigerator to soften and improve in flavour. Scoop into pretty stemmed glasses and top with cold Chocolate Sauce. Decorate with crystallised violets or chestnuts and serve with Cats' Tongues or Sponge Fingers.

Ginger Iced Cream *(serves 6–8)*

This is a delicious iced cream and ideal for serving at Christmas lunch as an alternative to Christmas pud. It is very good served with meringues flavoured with ground ginger.

4 eggs, separated
4oz (125g) caster sugar
1 teaspoon (1 x 5ml) ground
  ginger
2 tablespoons (2 x 15ml)
  brandy

¾pt (400ml) double or whipping
  cream
4 large pieces stem ginger,
  chopped
1oz (25g) chopped glacé cherries
  (optional)

Beat egg yolks with the sugar, ground ginger and brandy. Whip cream until it stands in soft peaks and add to the egg mixture. Whisk egg whites until stiff and fold into the mixture. Pour into a lidded container and freeze for about 1 hour. Add chopped stem ginger and glacé cherries and stir evenly into semi-set ice cream. return to freezer until completely set.

Remove from freezer to refrigerator 30 minutes before serving. Scoop out into pretty glasses, top with Chocolate Sauce or Butterscotch Sauce, and more chopped stem ginger or crushed Brandy Snaps.

Honey and Brandy Iced Cream *(serves 6–8)*

4 eggs, separated
4 tablespoons (4 x 15ml) warmed honey

3 tablespoons (3 x 15ml) brandy
¾pt (400ml) double or whipping cream

Beat egg yolks until pale in colour. Add warmed honey a little at a time, beating continuously. Add the brandy. Whip the cream until it stands in soft peaks and add to the egg mixture. Whisk egg whites until stiff and fold into mixture. Pour into a lidded container or individual pots and freeze. This recipe will make a softer iced cream which will not have to be taken out of the freezer until 15–20 minutes before serving. If you use individual pots they can be served straight from the freezer. Scoop out and serve with Butterscotch or Coffee Sauce and Brandy Snaps.

Marmalade Iced Cream *(serves 6–8)*
Any marmalade may be used in this recipe depending on your personal taste. Be careful to check for sweetness before adding sugar because the amount will vary with the kind of marmalade you use.

4 eggs, separated
1 tablespoon (1 x 15ml) lemon juice
4 tablespoons (4 x 15ml) marmalade

¾pt (400ml) double or whipping cream
4oz (125g) caster sugar

Beat egg yolks with the lemon juice. Stir in the marmalade. Whip the cream until it stands in soft peaks and add to egg mixture. Taste and add extra sugar as required. Whisk egg whites until stiff and fold gently into the mixture. Freeze in a lidded container. Serve with Lemon or Orange Sauce and Cats' Tongues.

Lemon and Elderflower Water Ice *(serves 6)*

Water ices and sorbets were served halfway through a heavy Victorian meal to refresh the palate and aid digestion. They were often flavoured with port, brandy, rum or fruit juice and spices. This ice has a delicious grapy taste and is very refreshing.

6oz (175g) honey or cube sugar
1pt (500ml) cold water

5–6 heads elderflower blossom
Grated rind and juice of 3 lemons

Put honey or sugar and water into a saucepan. Bring to the boil slowly, stirring to dissolve the honey or sugar. Boil rapidly for 5 minutes. Remove from heat, drop in flower heads, cover and leave to infuse for at least 30 minutes. Strain, add the lemon juice and lemon rind. Freeze in a lidded container until mushy. Stir to distribute the lemon rind evenly. Freeze again. It will take 4–5 hours to freeze completely. Serve in scoops in pretty glasses and topped with sprigs of fresh mint. Serve with Cigarette Biscuits or Cats' Tongues.

Melon Sorbet *(serves 6)*

4oz (125g) cube sugar
½pt (250ml) cold water
1½lb (675g) melon, very ripe

Juice of ½ lemon
1 tablespoon (1 x 15ml) rum
2 egg whites

Put sugar and water into a saucepan and bring to the boil slowly to dissolve the sugar. Boil rapidly for 5 minutes to make a syrup. Cool completely. Scoop out melon pulp and discard seeds. Mash or blend to a pulp and add lemon juice. Mix with the syrup and just before freezing add the rum. Freeze until mushy, about 3–4 hours. Beat until smooth and then fold in stiffly beaten egg whites. Freeze again for another 2 hours. Sorbet will then be ready to serve. Scoop out into balls and garnish with fresh mint.

Variation:
Melon and Ginger Sorbet
Replace lemon juice and rum with 2 tablespoons (2 x 15ml) syrup from a jar of preserved stem ginger. Stir in 2 pieces preserved stem ginger chopped finely when you add the stiffly beaten egg whites.

Nesselrode Pudding *(serves 6)*

This was invented in the nineteenth century by a Monsieur Mony, chef to the famous Count Nesselrode after whom it was named. It is reputed to be the most famous of the iced puddings, and was always produced at Christmas. Why not make one this Christmas to serve alongside the Traditional Plum Pudding? This recipe is based on one I found in an unusual recipe book called *The Ice Book* written by Thomas Masters, 1844. Originally, fresh chestnuts would have been used, but tinned unsweetened chestnut purée will do.

For the vanilla syrup:	2 egg yolks
2oz (50g) granulated sugar	2oz (50g) caster sugar
¼pt (125ml) water	½pt (250ml) single cream
Vanilla pod	8oz (225g) tin chestnut purée (unsweetened)
1oz (25g) candied peel, chopped	1 tablespoon (1 x 15ml)
1oz (25g) raisins	Maraschino
1oz (25g) glacé cherries, quartered	¼pt (150ml) double or whipping cream
1oz (25g) currants	

To make the vanilla syrup, bring water, sugar and vanilla pod slowly to the bowl, stirring to dissolve the sugar. Boil rapidly for 5 minutes. Remove from heat and cool. When completely cold, remove the vanilla pod. (This can be washed and used again, so it is not as expensive as it might seem.)

Poach candied peel, raisins, cherries and currants in the prepared vanilla syrup for a few minutes. Drain, reserving syrup, and leave to cool.

Make a custard by beating egg yolks with the sugar until thick and pale yellow in colour. Heat the single cream to simmering point in a heavy-based saucepan, and stir into egg mixture. Strain back into the saucepan and stir continuously over gentle heat until the mixture thickens enough to coat the back of a spoon. Do not allow to boil. Pour into a large mixing bowl and leave to cool.

Mix the chestnut purée with reserved vanilla syrup and add to cooled custard with Maraschino. Stir well and pour into a lidded container. Freeze for 1 hour and then remove. Whip the cream until it stands in soft peaks and add to semi-set iced cream together with prepared raisins and currants. Freeze again until firm.

Serve topped with vanilla-flavoured cream and decorate with crystallised violets and angelica. This pudding looks very attractive frozen in a mould, turned out and then decorated with piped cream and grated chocolate or glacé cherries, crystallised violets or apricots — make it as elaborate and decorative as you wish. For Christmas, try decorating with tree baubles, ribbon or tinsel.

Ratafia Iced Cream *(serves 6–8)*

This was a very popular ice cream in Georgian days. Almonds were used a great deal to flavour puddings and cakes so it was hardly surprising that these little almond-flavoured biscuits should be used in a recipe for iced cream.

4oz (125g) ratafia biscuits
¼pt (150ml) sweet sherry
4 eggs, separated
3oz (75g) caster sugar

¾pt (400ml) double or whipping
  cream
1oz (25g) chopped toasted
  almonds

Crush ratafia biscuits and soak in sherry for 20 minutes. Beat egg yolks and sugar until thick and pale yellow in colour. Whip cream until it stands in peaks and add to egg mixture. Fold in soaked ratafia biscuits. Whisk egg whites until stiff and fold into mixture. Freeze in a lidded container for about 1 hour and then beat mixture and add chopped toasted almonds. Replace in the freezer and leave to set completely.

30 minutes before serving, remove from freezer into refrigerator and leave to soften. Serve topped with Madeira Sauce or Apricot Sauce.

Prune Iced Cream *(serves 6–8)*

Any dried fruit can be used in this recipe.

8oz (225g) large dried prunes
¼pt (150ml) water
1 tablespoon (1 x 15ml) lemon
  juice
2in (5cm) cinnamon stick

4 eggs, separated
4oz (125g) caster or soft brown
  sugar
¾pt (400ml) double or whipping
  cream

Soak prunes overnight in water and lemon juice. Next day, simmer prunes in soaking liquid with cinnamon stick until they are soft. Discard cinnamon stick and leave liquid to cool a little. Remove stones from the prunes and liquidise or sieve to make a purée with their cooking liquor. Allow to cool completely.

Beat egg yolks with the sugar until thick and pale in colour. Whip the cream until it stands in peaks and add to egg mixture. Stir in prune purée. Whisk egg whites until stiff and fold into prune mixture. Pour into a lidded container and freeze.

30 minutes before serving, remove from the freezer and place in the refrigerator. Serve with rum-flavoured whipped cream.

Variations:
Use 8oz (225g) apricots instead of prunes.
Use 8oz (225g) apricots and 2oz (50g) ground almonds.

Iced Tea Cream *(serves 6)*
This was a very popular ice cream in Edwardian times and is certainly worth making for a change, especially now that tea has become such a fashionable drink again. You can use any tea you like, but Earl Grey does give a very good flavour. Also try varying the herbs or flavourings you add — orange rind, lemon balm or rosemary.

3 teaspoons (3 x 5ml) Earl Grey tea	3 egg yolks
1 strip ᵊmon rind or	4oz (125g) caster sugar
1 sprig mint	¼pt (150ml) double or whipping cream
¾pt (400ml) milk	

Bring tea, lemon rind or mint and milk gently to the boil. Remove from heat, cover and leave to infuse for 10 minutes. Strain, then reheat to simmering point.

Beat egg yolks and sugar until thick and pale in colour. Gradually stir the hot milk into egg mixture. Strain into a heavy-based saucepan and stir continuously over gentle heat until the mixture thickens enough to coat the back of a spoon. Do not allow to boil. Pour into a large mixing bowl and allow to go cold.

Whip cream until it stands in soft peaks and fold into custard. Pour into a lidded container and freeze for 1 hour. Remove and beat mixture thoroughly. Freeze for another hour and then beat again. Return to freezer and freeze completely. Serve with Lemon Sauce.

FRIED PUDDINGS

Fried puddings were some of the earliest puddings to be made as the method was so simple and they could be cooked directly over the fire. Eggs were mixed with flour to make pancakes although they were not considered important enough to be listed in recipe books. Some were made from egg whites only and these were much admired and served alongside fritters, sprinkled with sugar. The latter appeared regularly on medieval menus as part of the last course. Apple, parsnip and carrot fritters were the most popular.

In Tudor and Stuart days milk or water and spices were added to pancake batter, and in Georgian days cream was used to enrich the batter, as well as brandy. Fritters continued to be popular although again the batter was further enriched.

Heavy suet pudding mixtures were also fried as an alternative to boiling. The method was much faster and easier. The mixture was formed into small cakes or balls and fried or stewed in butter.

The important thing to remember when cooking fried puddings, is that the fat or butter must be at the right temperature, particularly when deep-frying. Also most must be prepared at the last minute, although if you have a freezer they can be frozen already cooked and just reheated.

Poor Knights of Windsor *(serves 6)*

A traditional pudding from Berkshire, where the alleged poverty of medieval knights was jokingly commemorated, consisting of bread, soaked in sherry or wine, eggs and cream, and fried. The recipe probably originated from France and was called *Pain Perdu* or 'Lost Bread'. It is an excellent way of using up left-over bread or rolls. Also known in Georgian times as Spanish Fritters.

6 thick slices white or French
    bread
2 eggs
2 teaspoons (2 x 5ml) caster
    sugar
¼pt (150ml) single cream or
    milk
Pinch of ground cinnamon

Grated rind of ½ lemon
2 tablespoons (2 x 15ml)
    Madeira or sweet sherry
Butter and oil for frying
Extra sugar and cinnamon for
    sprinkling
Orange or lemon wedges for
    serving

Remove crusts from slices of bread and cut each slice into 3 fingers. (If you are using French bread don't remove crusts and use whole.) Beat eggs and sugar together in a basin. Heat cream or milk until it just reaches boiling point. Cool a little before pouring on to egg mixture, beating continuously. Stir in cinnamon, lemon rind and Madeira or sherry.

Melt a little butter and oil in a heavy frying pan. Dip each finger or piece of bread into custard mixture and fry until golden brown and crisp. Drain on crumpled kitchen paper and keep warm until all the bread has been fried. Sprinkle with caster sugar and ground cinnamon. Serve on a clean white napkin with orange or lemon wedges or with Syrup Sauce, Lemon Sauce, Orange Sauce or Jam Sauce.

Apple Fritters *(serves 6)*

Egg-batter fritters have been popular since medieval days, especially apple fritters. A spit holding dates, figs and apples was often hung in front of the fire, and as they cooked, the fruit was basted with batter until a thick crisp crust was formed round it. Slices of meat, fish, poultry, vegetables, all kinds of fruit and even flowers, especially apple blossom, were all made into fritters — the name probably comes from the Norman French. It means *anything* that is dipped in batter and fried. However, the most common fritters in Britain were made with apples, although later, oranges, pineapple, bananas and pieces of pumpkin became popular. Fritters are best eaten very hot, straight from the frying pan. The fruit should be sliced thinly so that it cooks through. This recipe has salad oil and stiffly beaten egg whites added to the batter just before frying, which make the fritters crisp and light. To make them very special, try adding a little fruit liqueur to the batter. Experiment with other fruits such as rhubarb, peaches, apricots, pineapple and oranges.

4oz (125g) plain flour
Pinch of salt
½ teaspoon (½ x 5ml) ground
  cinnamon
¼pt (150ml) tepid water
2 tablespoons (2 x 15ml) orange
  liqueur
1 tablespoon (1 x 15ml) salad oil
4 medium cooking or crisp
  dessert apples
Grated rind and juice of
  ½ lemon

2oz (50g) icing sugar
6 tablespoons (6 x 15ml) apricot
  jam or thick orange
  marmalade
1oz (25g) caster sugar
2 tablespoons (2 x 15ml) water
Fat for deep frying (lard or oil)
2 egg whites
Caster or sieved icing sugar for
  dredging
Orange segments for serving

Sieve flour, salt and spice together into a basin. Make a well in the centre. Gradually blend in tepid water and 1 tablespoon (1 x 15ml) liqueur, followed by oil. Beat vigorously with a rotary hand or electric whisk to make a smooth, glossy batter. Cover and leave to stand in a cool place for at least 30 minutes, to allow starch grains in the flour to absorb water and swell.

Peel, core and slice apples in ¼in (6mm) thick slices. Mix together lemon rind and juice, 1 tablespoon (1 x 15ml) liqueur and sieved icing sugar. Add apple slices and coat evenly. In a heavy saucepan dissolve caster sugar and jam over a low heat. Dilute with water to make a syrup of coating consistency. Simmer syrup for 1 minute and keep warm. Coat each soaked apple ring in this syrup, allowing excess to drain off. Leave apple rings on one side to dry out a little.

When ready to cook fritters, heat fat for deep-frying to 375°F (190°C). As soon as a slight blue vapour rises from the surface of the fat it is hot enough. Test by dropping in a little batter, which will rise quickly if the fat is the correct temperature; if not, the batter will sink. Make sure your fat is absolutely clean and at least 3in (7½cm) deep. Whisk egg whites until very stiff and fold into prepared batter. Using cooking tongs or a long skewer, dip apple rings, one at a time, into batter, allowing excess to drain off. Lower carefully into hot fat and deep-fry until crisp and puffed, turning them over once or twice. Avoid frying too many fritters at once, because this cools the fat and does not allow room for fritters to expand properly.

When cooked, remove fritters from fat and drain on crumpled kitchen paper. Bring fat to correct temperature again before frying next lot of fritters. Serve immediately on a clean white napkin dredged with caster or icing sugar and decorated with a few fresh flowers. Accompany with a bowl of whipped cream and orange wedges or with a little warmed honey, Apricot Sauce or Orange Sauce.

Variation:
Elderflower Fritters
These are rather fun to make. Dip heads of elderflower blossom in fritter batter and fry as before.

Traditional Lemon Pancakes *(serves 6)*
Although probably not of English origin, pancakes have been established in England for so many centuries that they may be considered a national institution. They were originally a very thick round or 'froise' of egg and flour batter, flavoured with herbs and spices. When Lent was strictly observed, eggs and fatty foods were forbidden for forty days and so pancake making became associated with Shrove Tuesday in England, to use up any remaining eggs, butter and milk before the fasting. This custom is the only survival in England of the feasting and

merrymaking of the gay carnivals which take place on that day in all Catholic countries. Pancake races on Shrove Tuesday are still very popular.

4oz (125g) plain flour	½oz (12g) melted butter
Pinch of salt	Lard or butter for frying
Grated rind of ½ lemon	Caster sugar for sprinkling
1 egg	2 lemons for serving
½pt (250ml) milk or milk and water	

Sieve flour and salt together into a basin. Stir in lemon rind. Make a well in the centre and break in the egg. Beat well, incorporating the flour, and add half the liquid very gradually, beating all the time until a smooth batter is formed. Add remaining liquid a little at a time and beat until well mixed. Leave to stand for at least 30 minutes.

Stir melted butter into the batter just before cooking. Heat a very little lard or butter in a pancake or omelet pan until very hot. Spoon in a tablespoon of batter and tip the pan until batter covers its base. Cook until golden brown underneath. Turn over with a palette knife and cook the other side until golden. Turn out on to sugared greaseproof paper, sprinkle with caster sugar and a squeeze of lemon juice. Serve immediately with extra sugar and lemon wedges, or keep warm in the oven until needed.

Variations:
Orange Pancakes
Add grated rind of 1 orange to the batter and cook in the usual way. To serve, sprinkle with sugar and pour orange juice over the pancakes.

Pancakes Ornate
Spread cooked pancakes with jam, roll up and serve with cream. Traditionally, apricot jam was used.

Ginger Pancakes
Sieve 1 level teaspoon (1 x 5ml) ground ginger with the flour and cook pancakes in the usual way. Serve spread with whipped cream flavoured with a little chopped preserved stem ginger.

A Quire of Paper *(serves 6)*
Much admired by seventeenth- and eighteenth-century cooks, a quire of paper consisted of a pile of wafer-thin pancakes. The batter, rich with eggs and cream, was run as thinly as possible over the bottom of a heavy pan and cooked on one side only. The completed pancakes were dredged with caster sugar and laid evenly one upon another until the pile contained twenty. A wine sauce and melted butter were served

with the pancakes, which were cut into wedges like a cake.

This recipe will make a pile of about ten thin pancakes which can be spread individually with jam, jelly or fruit purée.

4oz (125g) plain flour
Pinch of salt
1oz (25g) caster sugar
2 eggs
2 egg yolks
Unsalted butter for frying

½pt (250ml) single cream or
half cream and milk
2 tablespoons (2 x 15ml) medium
sherry
Caster sugar for sprinkling

Sieve flour and salt together into a basin. Stir in the sugar. Make a well in the centre of the flour. Put eggs and egg yolks into the well and gradually mix eggs and flour together. Add cream (or cream and milk) gradually, beating well until a smooth batter is formed. Stir in the sherry to make a thin cream.

Heat a heavy-based pancake or omelet pan, brush with melted butter and add 1 tablespoon (1 x 15ml) of batter. Twist the pan until the bottom is evenly coated with batter and cook until pancake is golden brown on the bottom. Remove from pan or turn over and cook the other side. Keep warm in a clean tea towel. Make a stack of pancakes, filling them with jam and whipped cream or whatever you choose. Sprinkle liberally with caster sugar. Serve hot, cut in wedges.

Loganberry and Ginger Cream Pancakes *(serves 6)*

Batter puddings have been traditionally served with soft fruit in the main fruit-growing areas of Britain. In this recipe, loganberries are folded inside crisp pancakes and topped with ginger-flavoured cream. Raspberries, strawberries or blackberries can be used instead.

4oz (125g) plain flour
Pinch of salt
1 egg
½pt (250ml) milk
12oz (350g) fresh or frozen
loganberries
6oz (175g) caster sugar
½pt (250ml) double or whipping
cream

4 level teaspoons (4 x 5ml) icing
sugar
2 level teaspoons (2 x 5ml)
ground ginger
½oz (12g) melted butter
Butter for frying
1oz (25g) toasted flaked
almonds

Sieve flour and salt together into a basin. Make a well in the centre and break in the egg. Beat well and gradually add the milk a little at a time until batter is smooth and creamy. Cover and stand in a cool place for at least 30 minutes.

Make sure loganberries are clean and free of leaves and sprinkle with caster sugar. Whip cream until thick. Sieve in icing sugar and ground ginger and stir well. Put in a cool place.

When ready to make the pancakes, stir melted butter into the prepared batter. Heat pancake or omelet pan and add a knob of butter. When it is sizzling, pour in 1 tablespoon (1 x 15ml) batter and tip pan to coat evenly with wafer-thin batter. Cook until golden on the bottom, toss and cook on the other side. Keep warm, while you cook the rest of the pancakes. Fill with prepared loganberries and cream, and fold. Serve on a warm serving plate, topped with toasted flaked almonds.

New College Puddings *(serves 6)*
Traditionally first served at New College, Oxford, in the nineteenth century, they first appeared in a recipe book by Dr Kitchiner, dated 1831. They were basically suet puddings which were fried instead of boiled. This reduced the cooking time considerably. Oxford Dumplings were very similar.

4oz (125g) shredded suet
4oz (125g) fresh white
  breadcrumbs
2oz (50g) caster or soft brown
  sugar
½oz (12g) baking powder
Pinch of salt
½ teaspoon (½ x 5ml) grated
  nutmeg

Grated rind of 1 orange
4oz (125g) currants
1oz (25g) candied peel
3 eggs, separated
2 tablespoons (2 x 15ml) brandy
  (optional)
Butter for frying

Mix suet, breadcrumbs, sugar, baking powder, salt and spice with orange rind, currants and candied peel, stirring thoroughly. Beat egg yolks and mix with brandy, if using. Stir into pudding mixture. Whisk egg whites and gently fold into pudding which should be a soft dropping consistency. Melt some butter in a heavy frying pan and fry tablespoonfuls of pudding mixture in hot butter, flattening the mixture as you cook it (like a fish cake). Turn once, frying each side for about 6 minutes until brown. Serve hot, sprinkled with sugar, and with Custard Sauce.

A Sweet Omelet *(serves 4)* *

The ancestor of the British omelet, known as a 'herbolace', was a mixture of eggs and shredded herbs baked in a buttered dish. Cheese and milk were added later. This herbolace was replaced by the French *omelette* in the fourteenth century, referred to in many English recipes as an Aumelette or Alumelle, which gradually became omelet. The word *omelette* probably came from the word derived from Latin for a leaf or thin sheet which was lamella. Even as late as the middle of the seventeenth century, opinions were still varied as to whether the omelet should be cooked on one side only or turned over and cooked on both sides, like a pancake. Eventually, the former way won although a hot 'salamander' or iron was sometimes held over the top of the omelet for a few seconds.

The sweet omelet was very popular in Edwardian days and was often served as a country weekend treat, when the cook would prepare it while the guests were eating the main course. It would then be brought to the table, flaming with brandy or rum.

In this recipe the omelet is filled with apples, but you can use cherries, plums or apricots in the same way or just serve filled with jam which is the traditional way. Apricot jam was always used.

2 large cooking apples	2 tablespoons (2 x 15ml)
4oz (125g) butter	Calvados or rum
4oz (125g) caster sugar	5 eggs
¼pt (150ml) double or whipping	Pinch of salt
cream	

Peel, core and slice apples. Fry apples gently in 2oz (50g) butter, turning frequently until tender. Remove from heat and add 2oz (50g) caster sugar, double or whipping cream, and Calvados. Stir well.

Separate 2 of the eggs and beat egg yolks and 3 whole eggs together. Add salt and 1oz (25g) caster sugar. Whisk the 2 egg whites until stiff and gently fold into egg mixture.

In a frying pan melt the remaining butter. When light brown in colour, pour in egg mixture and cook over a moderate heat, mixing it well with a fork to allow uncooked egg to run on to the bottom of the hot pan. Cook until golden brown on the bottom and cooked on the top. (Sweet omelets, unlike savoury omelets, should not be runny on the top.) Spread apple mixture over the top, fold in half and slide on to a warmed plate. Sprinkle with remaining caster sugar and caramelise by placing the omelet under a very hot grill for a few minutes.

Another attractive way of finishing this omelet is to heat a skewer until it is red hot and then draw it over the top of the sugar-sprinkled omelet in a criss-cross pattern. (The sugar will caramelise in a lattice pattern.)

A Puffed Strawberry Omelet *(serves 2)* *

A fluffy sweet omelet flavoured with orange rind and orange flower water filled with fresh strawberries. This kind of omelet was known over one hundred years ago.

3 eggs, separated
2 level teaspoons (2 x 5ml) caster
   sugar
Grated rind of 1 orange
½ teaspoon (½ x 5ml) orange
   flower water (optional)
2 tablespoons (2 x 15ml) water

½oz (12g) butter
8oz (225g) sliced strawberries
1oz (25g) icing sugar
1 tablespoon (1 x 15ml) Grand
   Marnier (optional)

Whisk egg whites with caster sugar until stiff, but not dry. Beat egg yolks, orange rind, orange flower water, if using, and water until creamy. Melt butter in an omelet or small frying pan over a low heat. Fold egg whites carefully into yolks using a metal spoon. Be careful not to overmix. Tip omelet pan to coat sides with butter. Pour in egg mixture. Turn on grill to heat up. Cook egg mixture over a moderate heat until golden brown underneath and just firm to touch in the centre. Place under pre-heated grill and cook until just set. Spread with sliced strawberries and sprinkle with sieved icing sugar. Fold omelet and slide gently on to a hot serving plate. Dredge with more icing sugar. Warm the Grand Marnier in a small saucepan, pour over omelet and set alight. Take to table immediately while omelet is still flaming. Serve with sweetened whipped cream.

Variation:
A puffed lemon omelet
Replace 1 tablespoon (1 x 15ml) of the water with lemon juice, and use grated lemon rind instead of orange. Omit orange flower water and add a little more caster sugar. Serve without the strawberry filling. Set alight with brandy if you like.

FRUIT AND JELLIES

FRUIT

Fruit and nuts remained uncultivated long after cereals were sown and harvested in prehistoric Britain. The Romans introduced orchards and new economic plants — larger and sweeter apples, sweeter cherries and vines to southern England. Some of this fruit was preserved in honey or vinegar, or dried in the sun.

Orchards continued into the medieval period and new varieties of apple and pear were introduced from France. Other known garden or orchard fruit trees were plums, damsons, medlers, quinces and mulberries. Strange and exotic fruits like lemons, Seville oranges, pomegranates, raisins, currants, prunes, figs and dates had begun to arrive in Britain from southern Europe. These, particularly the dried fruits, were eaten in vast quantities by the wealthy. The poor ate them on festive occasions, such as Christmas. Fresh fruit was regarded with suspicion, so most fruits were roasted, baked or stewed in pottages.

The sixteenth century saw an upsurge of interest in fruit and fruit growing. The country was at last enjoying peace after prolonged civil war, and men had the time and inclination to cultivate their gardens. Many of the British gentry began to take an interest in horticulture and their gardeners were kept busy developing new varieties of fruit and vegetables. Market gardening proved lucrative, especially around London, and Covent Garden was established as London's fruit market. A wide range of fruits was being grown in southern and midland England — apples, pears, plums, cherries, peaches, gooseberries, grapes, mulberries, bilberries, strawberries, raspberries and red and blackcurrants. The apricot and the melon were also grown on a limited scale. By the end of the sixteenth century, apricots and quinces were being grown against south-facing walls, a practice which probably stemmed from Italy.

Further north, the climate imposed limitations and fruit was raised principally in the gardens of the gentry. There were parts of the northwest where even apples and plums were hardly known among ordinary people before the eighteenth century. In Scotland too, fruit was grown on a limited scale.

The medieval fear of uncooked fruit died hard and it was often blamed when a person fell ill suddenly. All through the sixteenth and seventeenth centuries, the best way to eat fruit was to cook it first with

sugar and spices. Apples, pears (wardens) and quinces were baked for
several hours in pies. Soft fruits were boiled and pulped to form
'tartstuff' for pies and tarts or to be mixed with cream in a fool or
similar creamy dish. These cooked fruits became an ingredient of
puddings and were preserved in numerous ways so that they could be
used all year round.

It was only in the eighteenth century that fresh fruit began to be
regarded as a safe and even healthy food, and its popularity has grown
from strength to strength up to the present day.

JELLIES

Jelly was an established feasting dish in medieval times. Later, it
became divided into savoury and sweet forms and in the Tudor and
Stuart days the sweet versions formed an important part of the
'banquet' course. This was the third and final course of a formal
dinner and a development of the earlier dessert of spiced cakes, wafers
and apples. The diners withdrew to another room to dine on fruit
tarts, preserves, jellies and sweet wine. Many of the gentry went as far
as building special banqueting houses in their parks to which their
guests went after the main courses had been eaten. The desserts
served became more and more elaborate.

Jelly was particularly fashionable in the seventeenth century in
making extremely decorative dishes and tableaux — fish swimming in
ponds of jelly, birds flying in skies of jelly, great mounds of fresh fruit
set in jelly and layers of almonds, raisins and candied fruits glistening
through clear jelly. Usually they were highly coloured — even blue —
and highly spiced. Wine jellies were very popular and later, jellies
were flavoured with lemon juice, grape juice, bitter oranges or
quinces. These fruit jellies were slow to gain popularity because the
emphasis was still on colour rather than flavour. Jellies were stiffened
originally with calves' feet or neatsfoot, and a little later with
hartshorn.

Moonshine *(serves 4–6)* *

This romantically named pudding is a lemony jelly, popular with seventeenth- and eighteenth-century cooks. Saffron would probably have been used to colour the jelly in the seventeenth century as highly coloured foods were extremely popular. Make it in a fancy Victorian mould if you have one.

4oz (125g) caster sugar	Juice of 2 lemons
Finely pared rind of 2 lemons	½oz (12g) powdered gelatine
1pt (500ml) cold water	¼pt (150ml) whipping cream

Put sugar, lemon rind and water in a saucepan. Bring to the boil and simmer for 15 minutes to allow lemon rind to infuse. Leave on one side to cool. Strain. Put strained lemon juice in a cup and sprinkle over gelatine. Place the cup in a pan of water and gently heat until the gelatine has melted. Strain through a warmed fine-mesh sieve into the cooled lemon syrup. Stir well to make sure gelatine is mixed in thoroughly. Leave to cool again and, when just beginning to set, whisk until jelly looks like snow. Turn into a wetted mould and refrigerate until set.

Turn out on to a pretty plate by dipping mould quickly in hot water. Whip cream until thick and decorate jelly. Serve chilled with Cats' Tongues or Shortbread Hearts.

Black Caps *(serves 6)* *

The primitive form of baked apples was an apple baked in its skin in the ashes of the fire. The skins were often burnt on one side, hence the name Black Caps. Baked apples, often baked in cider or wine, have continued to be a country favourite for centuries. They can be filled with any dried fruit and topped with honey, jam or marmalade. The secret of a good baked apple is to use a good quality cooking apple, preferably a Bramley, which is England's finest cooking apple.

It was first grown in Nottinghamshire by an innkeeper and butcher called Matthew Bramley from Southwell, and introduced commercially in 1876. The Bramley is one of the late croppers and is large with a shiny green skin. It is very crisp and cooks superbly.

6 large Bramley cooking apples	3oz (75g) soft brown sugar
2oz (50g) chopped dates	1 level teaspoon (1 x 5ml) ground
2oz (50g) sultanas	mace or mixed spice
2oz (50g) raisins	1½oz (40g) butter
1oz (25g) chopped almonds or	¼pt (150ml) sweet sherry or
hazelnuts	Madeira
Grated rind and juice of 1 orange	

Wash and core apples. Score skin around the middle of each apple to prevent it bursting during baking, and stand close together in a well-buttered ovenproof dish. Mix chopped dates, sultanas, raisins and chopped nuts with orange rind and juice. Pack centres of apples with this mixture. Mix brown sugar and spice together and sprinkle over each apple. Top with a knob of butter. Pour sherry or Madeira around apples and bake in the centre of a moderate oven (350°F, 180°C; Gas Mark 4) for 45–60 minutes, basting occasionally. Serve hot, topped with clotted cream and extra brown sugar, with Honey and Brandy Iced Cream, or Ginger Iced Cream.

Variations:
Iced Apples *
Prepare as for Black Caps, but remove apples from oven about 15 minutes before the end of the cooking time. Strip off the top half of the skin. Whisk 3 egg whites very stiffly and whisk in 3oz (75g) caster sugar. Whisk again until stiff and glossy and then gently fold in another 3oz (75g) caster sugar. Coat baked apples with this meringue and return to the oven for a further 15 minutes, until meringue is crisp and lightly browned.

Mrs Abbott's Yule Logs *
This recipe was given to me by a lady who belongs to a local Women's Institute. She understands that it came from an old monastery cook book.
   Stuff apple cavities with raisins and bake as before in ¼pt (150ml) water mixed with 2 tablespoons (2 x 15ml) golden syrup. When cooked, warm 1–2 tablespoons (1–2 x 15ml) whisky, brandy or rum and, just before serving, pour over baked apples and set alight. Carry immediately to the table. Serve with an ice-cold Hard Sauce.

Cherries in Red Wine *(serves 6)* *
Cherries were introduced into Britain in the thirteenth century.

2lb (900g) dark red cherries	1 dessertspoon – 1 tablespoon
1oz (25g) sugar	(1 x 10ml – 1 x 15ml)
Pinch of ground cinnamon	arrowroot
¼pt (150ml) red wine	1–2 tablespoons (1–2 x 15ml)
3 tablespoons (3 x 15ml)	water
redcurrant jelly	3–4 sugar lumps
Juice of 1 orange	1 orange
	½pt (250ml) double cream

Stone cherries and place in a saucepan with the sugar and cinnamon. Cover pan and heat gently until the juices run freely, about 7–10 minutes. By this time the cherries will be at boiling point. Remove from heat, drain cherries and turn into a serving bowl, reserving juice. Put the wine in the saucepan and boil rapidly until reduced by half.

Add the redcurrant jelly and orange juice and heat gently until the jelly has melted. Add the juice from the cherries. Dissolve 1 dessertspoon (1 x 10ml) of arrowroot in 1 tablespoon (1 x 15ml) of water and add this to the saucepan. Bring to boiling point again. The liquor should now be smooth and rich looking but not gluey. You may need more arrowroot — it really depends on the juiciness of your cherries. Pour juice over cherries and chill well.

Rub sugar lumps over the rind of the orange until they are orange-coloured and well impregnated. Crush them in a bowl and add the strained juice of the orange. Whip the cream lightly, until it will barely hold its shape. Fold in the orange syrup. Chill well. Serve separately or pour over the top of the cherries in their serving bowl. Decorate with orange rind and whole cherries. Serve with Macaroons.

Oranges in Cointreau *(serves 6)* *

3 large oranges	2 tablespoons (2 x 15ml)
Grated rind and juice of 1 orange	Cointreau or Grand Marnier
About 1oz (25g) caster sugar	½pt (250ml) whipping cream

Peel oranges and remove all the pith. Slice across oranges thinly and place slices in overlapping rows in a shallow glass bowl. Mix orange rind, juice, sugar and liqueur together and sprinkle over oranges. (You may need a little more sugar depending on the sweetness of the fruit.) Whip the cream until fairly thick and spoon over orange slices. Chill well before serving. Decorate with spirals of orange rind and crystallised mint leaves. Serve with Orange and Almond Crisps, Cats' Tongues, or Brandy Snaps.

Nectarines Baked in Cream *(serves 6)* *
This delicious fruit has been known in Britain since the early seventeenth century and was frequently grown in the walled gardens of the great houses. Luckily, nectarines seem to have become more popular again in the last few years and are now readily available. Peaches, pears and apricots are equally as good in this recipe.

6 fresh nectarines	1 vanilla pod
½pt (250ml) double cream	1oz (25g) toasted flaked almonds
4oz (125g) caster sugar	

Skin nectarines by dropping in boiling water for a few minutes. Remove stones by running a knife round the fruit and twisting the two halves in opposite directions. Place nectarine halves in a shallow ovenproof dish. Heat cream, sugar and vanilla pod together gently until the sugar has dissolved. Pour cream over nectarines (don't remove vanilla pod). Bake in the centre of a moderate oven (350°F,

180°C; Gas Mark 4) for 30–40 minutes or until the fruit is tender. Remove from oven and chill well.

Serve very cold, sprinkled with toasted flaked almonds. Decorate with a few crystallised rose petals or simple fresh flowers. This dish is also very good served with hot Chocolate Sauce dribbled over the cream. Serve with Sponge Fingers or Cats' Tongues.

Variation:
Creamy Nectarine Tart*
Line a 12in (30cm) flan tin with shortcrust pastry and bake blind for 10–15 minutes at (400°F, 200°C; Gas Mark 6). Fill cooked pastry case with nectarine mixture as above and bake for a further 30 minutes.

Figs Baked in Honey *(serves 4–6)**
In the past, figs have been much more popular in British cookery than they are now. They were ripened in sheltered gardens in the south of England, but only a few are harvested today. There is something rather luxurious about fresh figs for pudding.

1lb (450g) fresh figs	2 teaspoons (2 x 5ml) lemon juice
½pt (250ml) white wine	Strip of lemon peel
4 tablespoons (4 x 15ml) clear honey	½pt (250ml) whipping cream
	1oz (25g) toasted flaked almonds

Arrange figs closely together in a shallow covered ovenproof dish. Put wine, honey, lemon juice and lemon peel in a saucepan and heat gently until honey has dissolved. Pour over figs. Cover and bake in a fairly hot oven (400°F, 200°C; Gas Mark 6) until tender. (Cooking time will vary depending on whether your figs are green or purple.) Remove from oven and leave to cool.

Whip cream and pile on top of the figs when they are cold. Sprinkle generously with toasted flaked almonds and chill well before serving. Serve with Cigarette Biscuits or Cats' Tongues.

Variation:
Figs Baked in Claret*
Bake figs in claret instead of white wine and substitute 2 tablespoons (2 x 15ml) sugar for the honey.

Brandied Peaches *(serves 6)**
By the beginning of the eighteenth century, recipes for brandied fruit, one of the early ways of preserving, began to appear in Britain. Peaches, nectarines, apricots, cherries and grapes were packed into earthenware jars containing brandy and a little sugar syrup. The jars were sealed closely and the fruit was ready for future use.

Peaches were introduced into English gardens by the Romans. By the seventeenth century there were twenty-two varieties growing in England, and they were not considered to be the luxury they are now, although in very recent years they seem to be cheaper and more plentiful again.

6 fresh peaches	2in (5cm) piece of cinnamon
Boiling water to cover peaches	stick
Juice of 1 lemon	1 bay leaf
12 cloves	1oz (25g) butter
½pt (250ml) cold water	2 tablespoons (2 x 15ml) brandy
5oz (150g) granulated sugar	

Cover peaches with boiling water for about 2 minutes. Remove from the water, and skin. Halve and stone peaches. Brush all over with lemon juice to stop them discolouring. Stick a clove in each half. Put water, sugar, cinnamon stick, bay leaf and butter into a small saucepan. Bring slowly to the boil to dissolve sugar. When it has completely dissolved, boil for 5 minutes to make a sugar syrup. Place peaches in a shallow ovenproof dish. Add brandy to sugar syrup and pour over peaches. Cover and bake in the centre of a fairly moderate oven (325°F, 160°C; Gas Mark 3) for about 30 minutes, or until peaches are tender, but still hold their shape. Remove bay leaf and cinnamon stick and serve either hot or cold with whipped cream and Shortbread Hearts.

Pears in Nightshirts *(serves 6)* *

The nightshirts are made of meringue! Pears are poached in cider, set on a bed of apple pulp and coated with crisp, pale brown meringue. The combination of apples and pears is a very old one, as they were the first two fruits to be grown in Britain. The apple pulp would have been flavoured with quince and spices. If you have access to a quince tree, do try flavouring apple puddings with just a few small pieces of quince — they have a lovely honey flavour. This pudding is very suitable for a dinner party.

6 large firm dessert pears	2–3 cloves
¾pt (400ml) cider	3–4oz (75g–125g) caster sugar
1½lb (675g) cooking apples	3oz (75g) sieved icing sugar
½oz (12g) butter	6 egg whites
Grated rind of 1 lemon	Pinch of salt
1 tablespoon (1 x 15ml) lemon	12oz (350g) caster sugar
juice	2oz (50g) toasted flaked almonds

Peel pears, but leave on the stalks. Put the cider into a saucepan large enough to take the pears. Bring to the boil and lower pears gently into this liquor. Cover and simmer very gently for 30–35 minutes or until pears are translucent and just tender. While pears are cooking, make apple pulp. Peel, core and slice apples. Rub butter over the sides and the bottom of a saucepan. Add apple slices, lemon rind, lemon juice and cloves. Cover with buttered greaseproof paper and cook over a low heat for about 15 minutes until apples are soft and any liquid has evaporated. Stir gently from time to time. Remove cloves and beat the apples to a smooth thick pulp with a wooden spoon. Add sugar to taste. Pour into a buttered ovenproof dish large enough to take the pears, allowing room for meringue coating.

Drain cooked pears and roll each one in sieved icing sugar. Place pears on top of apple pulp. Whisk egg whites until very stiff. Add 6oz (175g) caster sugar and whisk until stiff and glossy. Fold in remaining 6oz (175g) caster sugar and spread or pipe a thick coating of meringue over pears. Bake in a fairly hot oven (400°F, 200°C; gas Mark 6) for 10–15 minutes or until meringue is crisp and light brown. Decorate stalk ends with leaves of candied angelica or crystallised mint or lemon balm leaves. Serve immediately, sprinkled with toasted flaked almonds.

Warden Pears *(serves 6)* *
Pears have been cooked in this way since the fifteenth century. Along with apples, pears were the first fruit trees grown in Britain, dating back to the Middle Ages. The first pears were called Wardens and were very large and hard with a bright green skin with black marks. They tasted rather like a quince, and as they were so hard, many recipes were devised to cook them, hence this fifteenth-century recipe.

6 cooking or firm dessert pears
4oz (125g) soft brown sugar
½pt (250ml) water
½pt (250ml) sweet cider

6 strips of lemon rind
1in (2½cm) stick of cinnamon
1oz (25g) toasted flaked almonds

Peel pears, leaving on stalks. Remove 'eyes' of pears, opposite stalk ends. Stand in a deep ovenproof dish with a lid. Sprinkle with brown sugar. Mix water and cider together and pour round pears. Add the lemon rind and the cinnamon stick. Cover with the lid and bake in a slow oven (300°F, 150°C; Gas Mark 2) for about 4 hours, until tender and translucent. (A friend of mine has an Aga and she bakes her pears *overnight* in the slow oven.)

Leave pears to cool in cooking liquor and then lift them carefully, using a draining spoon, into a shallow serving dish. Remove the lemon rind and cinnamon stick from the liquor and boil it rapidly in a saucepan until a thick syrup. Pour over pears and chill well.

Serve well chilled, sprinkled with toasted flaked almonds, and with cinnamon-flavoured whipped cream.

Prunes in Port *(serves 6)* *

These are a far cry from nursery 'prunes and custard'! Fruit has been cooked in wine for many centuries. The recipe is rather extravagant, but claret or burgundy can be used just as successfully, and pears or plums instead of prunes. These are very good served at Christmas time.

12 large prunes	2 bay leaves
½pt (250ml) ruby or tawny port	3oz (75g) cube sugar
Strip of lemon peel	2 tablespoons (2 x 15ml)
2in (5cm) stick of cinnamon	redcurrant jelly

Soak prunes in port overnight. Next day, drain prunes and put soaking liquor in a saucepan with lemon peel, cinnamon stick, bay leaves and sugar. Dissolve the sugar over gentle heat and when completely dissolved bring to the boil. Boil rapidly for 1 minute. Put soaked prunes in this liquor, cover with a lid, and poach for about 30 minutes or until tender. Remove prunes from syrup with a draining spoon and put in a pretty serving dish. Remove bay leaves, lemon peel and cinnamon from syrup, add redcurrant jelly and boil rapidly until syrup is reduced and of a coating consistency. Cool a little, then pour over prunes. Serve chilled with a bowl of whipped cream.

Summer Pudding *(serves 6)*

This pudding is delicious and is best made with a mixture of soft summer fruits — raspberries, redcurrants or blackcurrants, cherries and blackberries — but don't use too many blackcurrants as their flavour is rather strong and tends to overpower the other fruits. Summer pudding was traditionally served on farms in the summer when there was a glut of soft fruit.

2lb (900g) mixed soft fruit	6 slices white bread (preferably a
4–6oz (125–175g) caster sugar	large milk loaf)
2 tablespoons (2 x 15ml) Kirsch	½pt (250ml) double cream

Pick over fruit, removing any stalks and stones. Put cleaned fruit, sugar and liqueur in a large heavy saucepan and cook over very gentle heat for 3–5 minutes or until the sugar has dissolved and juices begin to run. Don't overcook the fruit or its fresh flavour will be spoiled. Taste and add more sugar if necessary. Leave to cool a little.

Lightly grease a 1½pt (750ml) pudding basin and line with 5 slices of crustless bread, overlapping each other, and seal well by pressing the edges together. Fill in any gaps with small pieces of bread, so that none of the juice can get through, reserving 1 slice of bread. Pour the warmed fruit into the bread-lined basin, reserving a little juice which you will need later. Cover with the last piece of bread and stand the basin on a dish. Press a saucer or plate, one which will just sit inside the top of the basin with a 2lb (900g) weight on it, on top of the pudding. Leave in refrigerator or in a cold place overnight.

Just before serving, unmould by placing a serving dish upside-down on top of the pudding. Invert both together, and give the basin a sharp shake. Spoon reserved juice over any white pieces of bread still showing. Serve very cold, decorated with whipped cream, or with a bowl of whipped cream separately.

Variation:
Spiced Winter Pudding
Soak 6oz (175g) dried apricots in 1pt (500ml) water overnight. Place the apricots and soaking liquor in a saucepan and bring to boil. Simmer uncovered for 10–15 minutes. Strain apricots, reserving liquor. Return ½pt (250ml) of liquor to saucepan with 12oz (350g) peeled, cored and sliced cooking apples, 2oz (50g) raisins and 1 level teaspoon (1 x 5ml) ground cinnamon. Cook until apples are soft. Add apricots. Put 2 tablespoons (2 x 15ml) warm water in a cup and sprinkle over 1½ level teaspoons (1½ x 5ml) powdered gelatine. Place cup in a small saucepan of hot water and heat gently to dissolve gelatine. Pour through a warmed fine-mesh sieve into the fruit mixture. (This ensures that any tiny lumps are removed. If the sieve is not warm a thin layer of gelatine will remain on it and then your pro-portions will be wrong.) Add 4–6oz (125–175g) caster sugar to taste and leave to cool a little.

Line and fill the basin as described above. Just befor serving un-mould and decorate with whipped cream and raisins. Serve very cold.

Raspberries in Strawberry Cream *(serves 4–6)* *
Raspberries were first recorded as a garden fruit in 1548. They are a very versatile fruit and freeze extremely well. Try reversing this recipe and serve fresh strawberries in raspberry cream.

1½lb (675g) fresh or frozen raspberries	12oz (350g) strawberries
4oz (125g) caster sugar	½pt (250ml) double or whipping cream
Juice of 1 orange	Icing sugar to taste
2 tablespoons (2 x 15ml) Kirsch	

Place raspberries, reserving a few berries, in a pretty serving bowl. Sprinkle with sugar, orange juice and Kirsch. Leave in a cool place while preparing the cream.

Rub strawberries through a sieve. Lightly whip the cream and fold in strawberry purée. Add sieved icing sugar to taste. Spoon this cream over the raspberries and chill well before serving. Decorate with reserved raspberries and crystallised mint leaves. Serve with Short-bread Hearts.

Strawberries in Orange Cream *(serves 4–6)* *

British strawberry plants were brought into the garden from the woodlands and improved by crossing with a larger variety from the continent, but the berries were still small. It was not until the nineteenth century that a further crossing with a Chilean strawberry and others produced the large strawberry we know today. History is amusing though, because we now treasure the little berries of the wild strawberry, which I am lucky enough to be able to gather a few yards from our farmhouse in Cornwall — they do have a very special flavour. Pears, peaches, apricots, loganberries, bananas and raspberries are all delicious served this way.

1½lb (675g) fresh strawberries
6oz (175g) ratafias
Grated rind and juice of
  2 oranges

2oz (50g) caster sugar
½pt (250ml) double or whipping
  cream

Hull strawberries, reserving a few of the best berries, and place in a pretty serving bowl with the ratafias. Moisten with the juice from 1 orange. Put grated rind, and juice of second orange, in a small basin. Add sugar and stir until dissolved. Whip the cream until it begins to hold its shape. Stir in orange syrup and taste to see if it is sweet enough. Add more sugar if necessary. Pile on top of the strawberries and chill for several hours before serving. Decorate with reserved strawberries, or with wild strawberries.

Clare College Mush *(serves 6)* *

Also called Eton Mess. The original recipe for this traditional pudding is said to have come from Clare College, Cambridge. It is a delicious combination of strawberries, cream and crushed meringues and can be flavoured with an orange liqueur, Kirsch, Framboise, brandy or vanilla.

2 large egg whites
4oz (125g) caster sugar
2lb (900g) fresh strawberries
1oz (25g) icing sugar

3 tablespoons (3 x 15ml) Kirsch
  or orange liqueur
¾pt (400ml) double or whipping
  cream

To make meringues, whisk egg whites in a clean bowl, with a balloon or rotary whisk. (Don't use an electric whisk, because it is very easy to overwhisk egg whites.) Whisk until whites are stiff enough not to fall out of the bowl when it is turned over. Add half the caster sugar and whisk again. Fold in remaining sugar. With a tablespoon, drop even amounts of meringue mixture on to a lightly greased baking tray. Bake in a very cool oven (250°F, 130°C; gas Mark ½) for about 1½hours, or until meringues are cream-coloured with a slightly soft chewy centre. Remove from the oven and leave to get cold.

Chop up strawberries roughly or leave whole if small. Save a few perfect berries for decorating. Sieve the icing sugar over strawberries and sprinkle with liqueur. Chill well for at least 1 hour.

Just before serving, whip the cream until it holds its shape. Gently fold in strawberries and their juices. Crush meringues into pieces and fold into cream and strawberry mixture. Taste, and add more sugar if necessary. Pile into a glass bowl and decorate with strawberries.

Port Wine Jelly *(serves 6)* *

½pt (250ml) cold water	1 bay leaf
4oz (125g) cube sugar	Grated rind of 1 lemon
1 tablespoon (1 x 15ml)	1 blade of mace
redcurrant jelly	½pt (250ml) ruby port
1in (2½cm) piece of cinnamon	1 tablespoon (1 x 15ml) brandy
stick	¾oz (18g) powdered gelatine
3 cloves	

Place cold water, sugar, redcurrant jelly, cinnamon stick, cloves, bay leaf, lemon rind and mace in a clean saucepan over gentle heat, stirring occasionally. When the sugar has completely dissolved and the jelly has melted, bring to the boil. Simmer for 10 minutes.

Put port and brandy into a second clean saucepan and heat gently. Sprinkle on the gelatine and bring to the boil. Simmer for 10 minutes.

Strain contents of both saucepans through a fine sieve into a large jug, stir, and as jelly cools pour into 6 goblets or pretty individual dishes, or into a wetted mould (if you want to turn jelly out). Leave to set in refrigerator.

Serve chilled. If you have used individual dishes or goblets, put them on a doyley-covered plate and decorate with a few fresh flowers. Unmould jelly if you have used one large mould by inverting mould on to a wetted serving plate. (You can then slide your jelly into the centre of the plate if it is not in the correct position.) If the jelly is difficult to get out of the mould, dip it quickly in hot water. Serve decorated with individual fresh flowers and with Shortbread Hearts.

MILK PUDDINGS, CUSTARDS AND TRIFLES

Milk puddings were developed from the cereal pottages of medieval times, and were originally cooked directly over the fire as they tended to be runnier than other puddings and therefore did not burn as easily. The new cereal of the later medieval period was rice imported from Italy on the spice ships and this, alongside sweetened milk pottages of crumbled bread, barley, oatmeal and wheat, was eaten on fasting days — the milk used was almond milk as milk from animals was forbidden.

Until the seventeenth century milk pottages continued to be eaten, on fasting days only, but eventually rice and sago puddings were accepted as supper dishes among the gentry. However, they were never classed with puddings in cookery books until modern times. A typical seventeenth-century 'rice pudding to bake' was made as follows: 'Boil the rice tender in milk, then season it with nutmeg, mace, rosewater, sugar, yolks of eggs, with half the whites, some grated breadcrumbs, and marrow and bake it in a buttered dish.' You can see from this recipe that milk puddings tended to be elaborate affairs and were highly flavoured with spices, rose-water or orange flower water. In Georgian times milk puddings were often baked in a pastry case and were rich with cream, eggs and dried fruit. Sometimes they were boiled in a well-buttered cloth instead of being baked.

For many centuries, custard has enjoyed great popularity in Britain, although the custard of our ancestors was very different from that of the modern housewife who usually makes it from a synthetic powder. The Romans brought with them the domestic hen and for the first time eggs were readily available. These were combined with milk to form a custard mixture which was cooked very slowly in an earthenware pot.

Custard continued to be eaten, the Elizabethans being particularly fond of it. It was usually served in a crust or mould of paste like our present-day custard pies and tarts. A favourite Elizabethan joke was 'The Almaine Leap into a Custard' — a jester suddenly entered the room where a meal was taking place and, springing over the heads of the astounded guests, plunged himself into an enormous dish of custard placed on the table. This joke was popular at the Lord Mayor's feast!

There are two types of custard: baked or steamed, and the softer pouring custard, which is used as a sauce. Egg whites set a baked custard and egg yolks give it a creamy consistency, but as the yolks thicken at a higher temperature than the whites, it is important to cook custards at the correct temperature. Too much heat, especially direct heat, will curdle an egg custard, so use a double saucepan, if you have one, for making a custard sauce, and stand a baked custard in a roasting tin half-filled with *cold* water. If you haven't a double saucepan, use a heavy-based saucepan with a film of cold water in the bottom over very gentle heat. Using a little cornflour in a custard sauce helps to prevent it curdling and, if the worst should happen, a curdled custard can often be rescued by turning it into a cold bowl and whisking like mad! Sieving will also help.

The original trifle of the Tudor and Stuart period was very different from our modern-day trifle. It was just thick cream heated until lukewarm with spices, usually ginger, sugar and rose-water. By 1751, trifle was being made with crumbled Naples biscuits, macaroons and ratafias soaked in sack at the bottom of the bowl, and these were covered with a rich custard and topped with syllabub. Later recipes replaced the syllabub with whipped or 'milled' cream, fruit or preserve was included and the modern trifle was established.

MILK PUDDINGS

Fine Almond Blancmange *(serves 4–6)* *
Although its actual name is undoubtedly of French origin, blancmange has been known in England for many centuries. It is mentioned in some of the oldest cookery books as 'Blewe Manger' or 'Blank Mange' or 'white food'. Chaucer, in *The Canterbury Tales*, describes it as a mixture of 'minced capon with flour, cream and sugar'. In fact, it was made with any white meat stewed with rice, dried fruits, almonds and spices. Exactly when the meat was omitted is not known, but by Elizabethan times the dish had become a mixture of cream, sugar and rose-water, thickened with egg yolks.

The English blancmange of the eighteenth century was a kind of jelly, stiffened with isinglass or hartshorn and flavoured with almonds and rose-water. By the early 1820s, arrowroot was being exported to Britain from the West Indies and became the thickening agent. Boiling milk, sweetened and seasoned with cinnamon, mace, and lemon peel, was poured on to a solution of arrowroot. It was set in elaborate moulds — and here was the true forerunner of our modern cornflour blancmange.

Try experimenting with different flavourings like chocolate, coffee, lemon, orange, brandy or other liqueurs and vanilla.

1½oz (40g) cornflour
½pt (250ml) milk
½pt (250ml) single cream
1 bay leaf
Strip of lemon peel

2 tablespoons (2 x 15ml) caster sugar
4–5 drops almond essence
1oz (25g) toasted flaked almonds

Mix the cornflour to a smooth paste with a little of the milk. Heat the rest of the milk and cream in a saucepan with the bay leaf and lemon peel and gradually blend in cornflour mixture. Bring to simmering point and cook for about 3 minutes, stirring continuously until thickened. Remove from heat and sweeten to taste. Stir in almond essence. Pour into a fancy 1pt (500ml) mould, rinsed out with cold water. Put in refrigerator to set. Unmould on to a pretty plate, decorate with toasted almonds and serve with Apricot Sauce and Almond Tiles.

Durham Fluffin' *(serves 6)* *
A milk pudding traditionally eaten in the north-east of England on Christmas Eve. The pearl barley has to be soaked in water overnight.

2 tablespoons (2 x 15ml) pearl barley, soaked overnight in water
1pt (500ml) milk
¾ teaspoon (¾ x 5ml) grated nutmeg

A few drops of brandy
2oz (50g) soft brown sugar or 1 tablespoon (1 x 15ml) honey
Crystallised orange slices for decorating

Simmer soaked pearl barley in the milk for about 30 minutes or until it is a smooth cream. Add grated nutmeg, brandy, and sugar or honey to taste. Serve hot in individual dishes with plenty of pouring cream, decorated with crystallised orange slices.

A Devonshire Junket *(serves 4)* *
This is a junket covered with clotted cream, popular in Devon and Cornwall — so simple, but so delicious. Junket has been made since the thirteenth century and is probably of Norman origin. Its name

comes from the word *jonquette*, French for the little rush baskets in which it was made. The original junket was a rich confection of cream, curdled with rennet, and flavoured with spices. Later, rose-water and orange flower water were added and junket was eaten alongside the jellies and flummeries as a sweetmeat or 'sublety' at the end of a meal. It was traditionally served in beautiful junket bowls with stewed fruit, but is especially good with fresh raspberries or strawberries.

1pt (500ml) fresh milk
2 tablespoons (2 x 15ml) caster
   sugar
1 teaspoon (1 x 5ml) rennet
1 tablespoon (1 x 15ml) rum or
   brandy

4oz (125g) clotted cream
½ teaspoon (½ x 5ml) grated
   nutmeg or ground cinnamon
1oz (25g) toasted flaked almonds

Heat milk gently in a heavy saucepan to blood temperature, or for about 5 minutes. Add half the sugar and stir until dissolved. Add rennet, stir lightly and stir in rum or brandy. Pour into a glass dish. Leave in a cool place, preferably not the refrigerator, for about 4 hours until set firm. Refrigerate for another hour.

Spread clotted cream on top of the junket. Sprinkle with grated nutmeg or ground cinnamon and remaining sugar. Serve sprinkled with toasted flaked almonds and with a bowl of fresh soft fruit, or with a fruit sauce. Accompany with Macaroons or Brandy Snaps.

Variation:
*Orange or Lemon Junket**
Add grated rind of 1 orange or lemon to the milk, and heat. Continue as before.

Spicy Ground Rice Pudding *(serves 4–6)**
This recipe is based on one by Eliza Acton, one of the best known of the nineteenth-century cookery writers. Eggs are added to make a richer pudding. Pies and puddings were often 'iced' or topped with egg whites as in this recipe.

1½oz (40g) ground rice or
   semolina
1pt (500ml) milk
Strip of lemon peel
1 vanilla pod
1 bay leaf
Pinch of ground nutmeg

1oz (25g) caster sugar or ½
   tablespoon (½ x 15ml) honey
2 eggs, separated
1oz (25g) butter
Grated nutmeg or ground
   cinnamon for sprinkling
4oz (125g) caster sugar

Butter well a 2pt (1 litre) ovenproof dish. Mix ground rice or semolina to a smooth paste with a little of the milk in a basin. Boil the rest of the milk with the lemon peel, vanilla pod, bay leaf and pinch of nutmeg.

Pour on to ground rice or semolina, stirring continuously. Rinse the pan in which the milk was boiled and leave a film of cold water on the bottom. Return rice and milk and bring slowly to the boil again, stirring all the time, so that it does not burn on the bottom of the saucepan. Cook gently for 10 minutes. Add the sugar or honey. Beat egg yolks and beat into rice. Remove vanilla pod, bay leaf and lemon peel. Pour into prepared pie dish. Dot with butter and sprinkle with nutmeg or cinnamon. Bake in the centre of a moderate oven (350°F, 180°C; Gas Mark 4) for about 25 minutes. Whisk egg whites until stiff and whisk in 2oz (50g) caster sugar. Fold in another 2oz (50g) caster sugar. Pile the sweetened egg whites on top of the pudding and bake for a further 20 minutes until meringue is crisp and lightly browned.

Serve hot with pouring cream and a fruit sauce.

Variations:
Try edging pie dish with puff pastry.
Add 2oz (50g) currants, sultanas or raisins and 1oz (25g) candied peel.

Queen's Pudding *(serves 6)*
Also called Queen of Puddings, it was named after Queen Victoria and was created by her chefs at Buckingham Palace, but it was, in fact, based on a much older seventeenth-century recipe — a milk pudding thickened with breadcrumbs and eggs. It was originally baked in a 'puff paste' case. Try using lemon or lime curd instead of jam.

3oz (75g) fresh white breadcrumbs	Grated rind of ½ lemon
3 eggs, separated	3 tablespoons (3 x 15ml) raspberry or strawberry jam
7oz (200g) caster sugar	Glacé cherries and candied
1pt (500ml) milk	angelica for decorating
1oz (25g) butter	

Butter a 2pt (1 litre) ovenproof dish. Sprinkle breadcrumbs in the bottom of the dish. Beat egg yolks with 1oz (25g) caster sugar. Put milk, butter and grated lemon rind into a saucepan and bring slowly to the boil. Leave to cool a little and then pour on to egg yolks, stirring continuously until mixture is smooth. Strain the custard over breadcrumbs and leave to soak for at least 15 minutes. Stand dish in a roasting tin half-filled with hot water and bake in the centre of a moderate oven (350°F, 180°C; Gas Mark 4) for 25–30 minutes, or until lightly set. Warm the jam and spread over the top of the pudding. Whisk egg whites until very stiff and add 3oz (75g) caster sugar. Whisk again until stiff and glossy. Fold in remaining sugar. Pile or pipe meringue on top of jam. Sprinkle with extra caster sugar and bake for a further 15–20 minutes or until meringue is crisp and lightly browned.

Serve hot with pouring cream or Jam Sauce, decorate with glacé cherries and candied angelica. This pudding is also delicious served cold with a bowl of fresh raspberries or strawberries.

Variation:

Manchester Pudding*

Put a layer of apricot jam in the bottom of an ovenproof dish. Continue as before, but include 2 tablespoons (2 x 15ml) sherry or brandy in the custard. When the pudding is lightly set, spread with more apricot jam, and top with meringue as before. Serve cold with pouring cream and Apricot Sauce.

Queen Mab's Pudding *(serves 4–6)**

This pudding is based on a recipe by Eliza Acton, author of *Modern Cookery,* published in 1845. It is really a custard, set with gelatine, with candied fruits added to make it richer. Candying was a method of preserving fruit, popular in Tudor and Stuart days. Whole fruits were candied and served at the banquet course after the main meal, as well as being chopped and used in cakes, puddings and biscuits.

1pt (500ml) milk	2 tablespoons (2 x 15ml) warm
1 bay leaf	water
1 vanilla pod	¾oz (18g) powdered gelatine
Strip of lemon peel	2oz (50g) chopped glacé cherries
2 large eggs, separated	1oz (25g) chopped candied
1½oz (40g) caster sugar	citron peel

Put milk, bay leaf, vanilla pod, and lemon peel in a saucepan and bring slowly to the boil. Remove from heat and cool a little. Beat egg yolks and sugar together and pour on flavoured milk, stirring continuously. Remove bay leaf, vanilla pod and lemon peel. Rinse milk pan with cold water, leaving a film of water on the bottom, and return milk and egg mixture to pan. Heat gently, stirring all the time and cook until thick enough to coat the back of a wooden spoon. Remove from heat.

Put warm water in a cup and sprinkle over gelatine. Place the cup in a pan of water and heat gently until the gelatine has dissolved. Pour through a warmed fine-mesh sieve into the custard. Whisk egg whites very stiffly and fold into cooled custard. Pour into a wetted mould and leave in a cool place until almost set. Stir in chopped cherries and peel and refrigerate to set completely.

Serve with a fruit sauce poured around pudding.

An Old English Baked Rice Pudding *(serves 6)* *

In Georgian times a rice pudding could be a very elaborate dish. It was either tied loosely in a cloth, boiled and eaten with melted butter, sugar or salt, or a richer dish including eggs, cream, butter, marrow, currants, brandy, ratafia, nutmeg and candied peel was baked with 'a paste round the edge'. This recipe is based on the second version. Try putting a puff-pastry edge round your pie dish and an inch or two (2½–5cm) below — it looks very effective.

2oz (50g) short-grain rice
¼pt (150ml) cold water
½pt (250ml) milk
½pt (250ml) single cream
1oz (25g) caster sugar, or ½
    tablespoon (½ x 15ml) honey
1 vanilla pod
1 bay leaf
1oz (25g) butter
¼ teaspoon (¼ x 5ml) ground
    cinnamon

¼ teaspoon (¼ x 5ml) ground
    nutmeg
2oz (50g) currants or sultanas
1oz (25g) candied peel
    (optional)
2 tablespoons (2 x 15ml) sherry
    or brandy
2 eggs, separated
1oz (25g) caster sugar

Wash rice and swell by adding cold water and boiling for 5 minutes. Drain, if necessary, and put in a buttered 2pt (1 litre) pie dish. Stir in milk, cream and 1oz (25g) sugar or honey. Add vanilla pod and bay leaf. Dot with butter and sprinkle half the spices over the top of the rice. Bake in the centre of a slow oven (325°F, 160°C; Gas Mark 3) for about 2 hours.

Remove dish from the oven, cool for 5 minutes, then stir in currants and peel, if using, and sherry or brandy. Remove vanilla pod and bay leaf. Beat egg yolks and add lightly to the rice mixture. Return to the oven for another 30 minutes.

Whisk egg whites until stiff. Whisk in 1oz (25g) caster sugar until smooth and glossy. Remove pudding from the oven and cool for 5 minutes. Gently fold in egg whites and sprinkle top with remaining spice. Return pudding to the oven for a further 15 minutes to set egg whites.

Serve hot with Jam, Marmalade, Red Cherry or Raspberry Sauce.

Variations:
Try adding chopped glacé cherries or grated apple.

Iced Rice Pudding
Use the 2 egg whites to make a meringue topping whisking them with 4oz (125g) caster sugar. Pile on top of rice pudding and return to oven as before.

Rice Creams *(serves 4–6)* *

This delicate creamy pudding can be served with fresh soft fruit or any fruit sauce. It is basically a cold rice pudding, mixed with cream, but this description doesn't do it justice!

2oz (50g) short-grain rice
½pt (250ml) creamy milk
1oz (25g) caster sugar
1 vanilla pod
1 bay leaf

1 level teaspoon (1 x 5ml)
   powdered gelatine
2 eggs, separated
½pt (250ml) double or whipping
   cream

Wash the rice in cold water, drain and put in a heavy saucepan with the milk, sugar, vanilla pod and bay leaf. Cook over gentle heat, stirring now and again to stop rice sticking on the bottom of the pan, until tender, about 40–45 minutes.

Remove from heat and take out vanilla pod and bay leaf. Sprinkle the gelatine into the hot rice and stir until dissolved. Beat egg yolks with 1 tablespoon (1 x 15ml) cream and stir into rice. Return the pan to the heat for a few minutes, and then place in a bowl of cold water. Stir until cool, but not set.

Whip remainder of the cream, until it begins to ribbon but does not stand in peaks. Whisk egg whites until very stiff. Fold cream into cool rice, followed by egg whites. Pour into individual glasses and chill well before serving. Decorate with a few raspberries or strawberries and place glasses on doyley-covered saucers covered with a fern leaf or strawberry leaves.

CUSTARDS AND TRIFLES

Caramel Pudding *(serves 6)* *

This is a very elegant pudding which appeals to even the most jaded of appetites. The custard pudding is covered with a beautiful caramel sauce, and is delicious served with fresh strawberries or raspberries.

4oz (125g) lump sugar
4 tablespoons (4 x 15ml) cold
   water
1 teaspoon (1 x 5ml) boiling
   water
1pt (500ml) milk
1 vanilla pod

1 bay leaf
2 eggs
3 egg yolks
2 tablespoons (2 x 15ml) caster
   sugar
1 tablespoon (1 x 15ml) brandy
   (optional)

Put oven on at 325°F (160°C; Gas Mark 3). Warm a 6in (15cm) soufflé dish, or a 6in (15cm) cake tin or a fluted mould (this makes a very attractive pudding) in the oven. You can also use individual moulds.

Put sugar and cold water in a heavy-based saucepan. Heat gently until the sugar has dissolved. Bring to the boil and boil rapidly without stirring until a rich brown caramel. Remove from heat, add a teaspoon (1 x 5ml) of boiling water and pour into warmed dish or mould. Using oven gloves or a tea towel, tip mould carefully to coat the bottom and sides with hot caramel. Leave to get cold.

Heat the milk with the vanilla pod and bay leaf. Leave to stand for 30 minutes to infuse. Bring to the boil and remove vanilla pod and bay leaf. Beat eggs, egg yolks and sugar together until pale in colour. Pour cooled milk on to egg mixture a little at a time to avoid curdling eggs, stirring continuously. Stir in brandy, if using. Strain custard into prepared mould. Stand in a roasting tin half-filled with hot water and bake in the centre of a pre-heated oven for about 45 minutes (30 minutes for individual moulds) or until custard is set. Cooking time will vary depending on the mould you have chosen to use.

When cooked, remove pudding from the oven, leave to cool completely and refrigerate before unmoulding. To unmould, loosen the edges of the pudding with the point of a knife. Place a shallow serving dish over mould and turn out quickly. Serve chilled with soft fruit.

Variations:
Try flavouring with coffee, chocolate, orange or lemon for a change.

Wine and Honey Cream
Make as before, but use sweet white wine instead of milk. Omit vanilla pod and bay leaf. Use honey instead of sugar.

Little Chocolate and Orange Pots *(serves 6)* *

6oz (175g) good quality plain chocolate	1 tablespoon (1 x 15ml) Cointreau or Grand Marnier
2 tablespoons (2 x 15ml) water	Grated rind of 1 orange
½oz (12g) butter	3 eggs, separated
	¼pt (150ml) double cream

Break chocolate into small pieces and put in a basin with the water over a pan of gently simmering water. Melt chocolate to a thick cream, slowly stirring from time to time. Remove from heat and stir in butter, orange liqueur and orange rind. Beat in egg yolks one at a time, stirring well after each addition (the egg yolks will be slightly cooked in the hot chocolate mixture). Leave to cool. Whisk egg whites until stiff, then stir briskly into chocolate. When thoroughly mixed, pour into custard pots or small dishes. Chill overnight.

Before serving, decorate with piped whipped cream and a piece of crystallised orange, or sprinkle with toasted flaked almonds or orange rind. Serve each pot on a pretty paper doyley, trimmed with a few fresh flowers such as rosebuds, freesias or marigolds. Accompany with Sponge Fingers or Cats' Tongues.

Variations:
Little Chocolate Pots *
Omit orange rind and orange liqueur.

Little Coffee and Chocolate Pots *
Add 1 tablespoon (1 x 15ml) coffee essence instead of orange liqueur and omit orange rind.

Floating Islands *(serves 6–8)* *
This elegant rose-flavoured pudding was a very popular dish in Georgian days. Fruit or sweetmeats decorated the edges and, according to Hannah Glasse, a cookery writer in the eighteenth century, it 'looks pretty in the middle of a table with candles round it'! She was absolutely right, because it is an extremely pretty pudding, consisting of a rich custard covered with poached meringues (the islands). Also known as Snowy or Snow Eggs.

1pt (500ml) double cream or milk	1½pt (750ml) water or water and milk
6 egg yolks	1 vanilla pod
2 level teaspoons (2 x 5ml) cornflour	4 egg whites
6oz (175g) caster sugar	Pinch of salt
1 tablespoon (1 x 15ml) rose-water	Crystallised rose petals
	Toasted flaked almonds

Bring cream gently to the boil in a heavy saucepan. Remove from heat and leave to cool a little. Cream egg yolks, cornflour and 2oz (50g) sugar together until almost white. Pour the hot cream over egg yolk mixture, gradually, beating well all the time. Rinse out the saucepan leaving a film of cold water on the bottom. Return custard to the saucepan and heat gently, stirring continuously until thick enough to coat the back of a wooden spoon. (Don't bring to the boil or the mixture will curdle.) Remove from heat immediately and leave to cool a little before stirring in the rose-water. Strain into your prettiest, shallow serving bowl, sprinkle with caster sugar to prevent a skin forming and leave to cool.

To make the 'islands', fill a shallow pan (a frying pan or poached-egg pan will do) with water or a mixture of milk and water, flavoured with a vanilla pod, and bring to simmering point. Whisk egg whites with a pinch of salt until stiff peaks. Whisk in 4oz (125g) caster sugar gradually, until smooth and shiny. Remove vanilla pod from the pan. Using a tablespoon (1 x 15ml) rinsed in cold water between each addition, spoon 4 'islands' into the pan of simmering water. Poach on each side for 2 or 3 minutes, until firm. Remove each 'island' with a draining spoon and drain on a clean towel. Repeat until meringue mixture is used up (you will make about 8 'islands'). Leave to cool. Arrange 'islands' carefully on the 'lake' of custard, and chill. Just before serving, sprinkle with crushed crystallised rose petals and toasted flaked almonds.

Variation:
*Caramel Floating Islands**
Make the dish in exactly the same way as before, but instead of decorating with rose petals and almonds, dissolve 3oz (75g) sugar in 2 tablespoons (2 x 15ml) water and boil rapidly until a rich golden brown. Remove from heat and trickle over the 'islands'.

A Gooseberry Trifle *(serves 6)**
In this recipe, gooseberry pulp has replaced the more usual sponge cake at the bottom of the trifle, and is covered with a rich custard and topped with a 'whip' which was a Victorian version of syllabub. If possible, make the syllabub topping a day in advance. Any fruit pulp can be used.

The topping:	1½lb (675g) green gooseberries
Grated rind and juice of 1 lemon	3 tablespoons (3 x 15ml) cold
6 tablespoons (6 x 15ml) sweet	water
white wine or sherry	9oz (250g) caster sugar
2 tablespoons (2 x 15ml) brandy	½pt (250ml) double cream
2oz (50g) caster sugar	Strip of lemon peel
½pt (250ml) double cream	4 egg yolks
	1 level teaspoon (1 x 5ml)
	cornflour

Put lemon rind and juice into a small bowl. Stir in wine or sherry, brandy and sugar until the sugar has dissolved. Cover and leave for several hours to infuse.

Strain the liquid into a clean bowl and stir in cream gradually, beating until it almost reaches a soft peak stage. (Don't use an electric beater. If overbeaten, syllabub will become grainy.) Chill overnight.

Next day, top and tail gooseberries and put in a heavy saucepan with the water and 2oz (50g) sugar. Simmer gently for about 20 minutes until soft. Rub through a sieve or beat to a pulp. Add 6oz (175g) sugar — you may need more, if gooseberries are tart. Put in a pretty shallow bowl and leave to cool.

Bring ½pt (250ml) double cream slowly to the boil with strip of lemon rind, and leave on one side to cool a little. Cream egg yolks, cornflour and 1oz (25g) caster sugar together until almost white. Remove lemon rind and pour on the hot cream in a steady stream, beating all the time. Rinse out the saucepan used for heating the cream, leaving a film of water in the bottom. Return egg mixture to pan and heat gently until thick enough to coat the back of a wooden spoon. (Don't boil because the custard will curdle.) Remove from heat and leave to cool. Pour over gooseberry pulp. Sprinkle with caster sugar to stop a skin forming and leave to get completely cold.

Pile prepared syllabub on top of the custard and chill well. Just before serving, decorate with twists of lemon rind or lemon slices and sprigs of fresh rosemary. Serve accompanied by Sponge Finger Biscuits, or Cats' Tongues.

Butter'd Oranges *(serves 6)* *
Custard made with butter and eggs was a popular pudding during the seventeenth and eighteenth centuries. This recipe is more like an orange cheese or curd rather than a custard. It is very rich but also refreshing. You can serve in empty orange skins if you wish. (It is always worth freezing spare citrus fruit skins if a recipe calls for just the flesh and juice — they can be filled with custard as here, or with water ice, sorbet, rice cream or fruit jelly.)

Thinly pared rind of 2 oranges	3 egg whites
Juice of 1 orange	8oz (225g) unsalted butter
1 tablespoon (1 x 15ml) concentrated frozen orange juice (thawed)	1 large piece candied orange peel
	¼pt (150ml) whipping cream
2oz (50g) caster sugar	Crystallised angelica and orange slices
4 egg yolks	

Put orange peel in a small saucepan of boiling water and boil for 20 minutes or until soft. Drain and purée peel in a blender or pass through a food mill or just pound orange peel with a rolling pin. Add orange juices and sugar to peel and beat until the sugar has dissolved. Add egg yolks and egg whites and whisk until mixture is thick and smooth. Melt the butter and leave until cool, but not beginning to harden. Pour butter in a steady stream into egg and orange mixture and blend in a liquidiser for about 3 minutes, or beat with a rotary whisk for about 10 minutes. Refrigerate, beating occasionally until thick and beginning to set. Cut candied orange peel into tiny pieces, or shred with a grater. Fold into half-set orange custard. Pour into individual glasses or custard pots and chill well. Decorate, before serving, with whipped cream and crystallised angelica and orange slices. Serve with Orange and Almond Crisps or Cats' Tongues.

Old English Sherry Trifle *(serves 6–8)* *

Sometimes I put a syllabub topping on trifle instead of cream — it is absolutely delicious and very rich.

For the base:

2 x 7in (17½cm) fatless sponge cakes or 1 packet sponge cakes	4oz (125g) ratafias or macaroons
1lb (450g) apricot jam, apple or quince jelly	¼ bottle medium dry sherry or Madeira

For custard and topping:

1pt (500ml) milk or cream	2 teaspoons (2 x 5ml) cornflour
Vanilla pod, pierced	6 egg yolks
2oz (50g) caster sugar	1pt (500ml) double cream

For decoration:

4oz (125g) glacé cherries	2oz (50g) crystallised pineapple
4oz (125g) blanched almonds	4oz (125g) ratafia biscuits
2oz (50g) crystallised apricots	Crystallised angelica leaves
2oz (50g) crystallised chestnuts	

Split sponge cakes or sponge bases in half, and liberally spread with chosen preserve. Sandwich together and cut into 1in (2½cm) fingers. Arrange in your prettiest shallow dish — you will need one about 12in (30cm) across the top and 3in (7½cm) deep. Sprinkle with ratafias or macaroons and plenty of sherry or Madeira and set aside.

To make the custard, bring milk or cream with vanilla pod to the boil. Mix sugar with cornflour, add egg yolks gradually and beat well until smooth. Remove vanilla pod from the milk and pour on to the egg mixture, stirring all the time. Rinse out the milk pan, leaving a film of cold water in the bottom. Return custard to the pan and stir well with a wooden spoon over a low heat until thick. Plunge the bottom of the pan, immediately the custard is thick enough, into a bowl of cold water to stop mixture curdling. Leave to cool a little.

When the custard is fairly cool, pour over the sponge, and leave to cool completely. When cool, whip cream until it stands in peaks and spread a thick layer over the custard. Pipe the top with remaining cream and decorate with loads of crystallised fruits and nuts and ratafias — the more the merrier, especially at Christmas!

To serve at other times of the year, this trifle can be decorated with crystallised flowers, a full-blown crystallised rose or just rose petals.

Sussex Tipsy Cake *(serves 6–8)* *

Also known as Hedgehog, this is a sponge cake that was traditionally soaked in as much brandy as it could absorb. Blanched almonds cut into spikes, hence the hedgehog, were then stuck into the sponge and a rich egg custard was then poured over and around it. In the nineteenth century it was more usual to use sweet white wine and lemon juice instead of brandy.

1 x 7in (17½cm) Victoria sponge cake	6 egg yolks
Raspberry jam for filling sponge	2–3 drops of almond essence
½pt (250ml) sweet white wine	2oz (50g) caster sugar
Juice of 1 orange	2 teaspoons (2 x 5ml) cornflour
2oz (50g) blanched almonds	3 tablespoons (3 x 15ml) single cream
1pt (500ml) milk	2 tablespoons (2 x 15ml) brandy
1 vanilla pod	

Fill sponge cake with raspberry jam. Pierce several times right through the cake with a skewer. Place the cake on a pretty serving dish or cake stand and pour over wine and orange juice, a tablespoon (1 x 15ml) at a time, letting it soak in. Cut blanched almonds into slivers or spikes and stick them into the top of the cake so that it bristles like a hedgehog.

Put milk and vanilla pod in a saucepan and bring to the boil. Set on one side to cool a little. Beat egg yolks, almond essence and sugar in a basin. Mix in the cornflour to a smooth paste. Remove vanilla pod from the milk and pour on to the egg mixture, stirring all the time. Rinse out the milk pan, leaving a film of cold water in the bottom. Return custard to the pan and stir well with a wooden spoon over a low heat, until it is thick and coats the back of the spoon. As soon as the custard has thickened, stir in cold cream to prevent it cooking any further and curdling. Leave to cool a little.

Just before serving, pour brandy over the cake, letting it soak in completely, then spoon over waiting custard. Serve immediately with whipped cream.

Trinity Pudding *(serves 6–8)* *

This pudding, also known as Burnt Cream and Cambridge Cream, was traditionally served during May week at Trinity College, Cambridge, for dinner. It was brought in on a large silver dish and the caramelised top was cracked with great ceremony.

The recipe is said to have been based on a very ancient Scottish dish which may have been brought over to Britain from France by Mary, Queen of Scots. It is similar to the delicious French *Crème Brulée*. There are endless versions of this creamy pudding with different flavourings — lemon rind, vanilla pod, or a bay leaf. The sugary top used to be browned by a 'salamander', a flat iron which was heated and passed over the top of the pudding.

You can make this custard in one large baking dish or individual ovenproof dishes, and it is best made the day before you want to serve.

1½pt (750ml) double cream	3oz (75g) caster sugar
1 vanilla pod	Caster sugar for caramelising
6 egg yolks	

Put cream and vanilla pod into a saucepan and bring very gently to the boil. Leave to cool a little. Remove vanilla pod, wash and reserve for future use. Cream egg yolks and sugar together in a basin until almost white. Pour hot cream on to yolks in a steady stream, whisking all the time. Strain into a shallow ovenproof dish, or individual dishes, and place in a roasting tin half-filled with hot water. Bake in a slow oven (300°F, 150°C; Gas Mark 2) for 1–1¼ hours or until just set. Remove dish and leave until cold. Chill in refrigerator overnight, if possible.

Just before serving, coat the top of the pudding with an even layer about ¼in (6mm) thick of caster sugar, using a sugar dredger. Heat the grill until really hot. Put the pudding in a roasting tin or large dish of ice cubes. (This will make sure that your custard does not spoil when you are caramelising the top.) Slip under the hot grill and watch carefully, turning if the sugar is browning unevenly. When the sugar has completely melted and is an even caramel colour, remove the tin and leave to cool.

Serve chilled, placed on a doyley-covered plate or a clean white napkin, decorated with a few fresh flowers. Serve with a bowl of fresh cherries, strawberries or raspberries when in season.

Her Majesty's Pudding *(serves 6–8)* *

Originally, this pudding would have been baked in a pastry case, hence the Custard Tart or Sweet Egg Pie. From the late seventeenth century, the custard was frequently separated from its pastry case and baked and served by itself — in a deep dish at first and then in special custard cups.

1oz (25g) unsalted butter	1 bay leaf
5 eggs	Strip of lemon peel
2oz (50g) caster sugar	1 tablespoon (1 x 15ml) brandy
1pt (500ml) single cream or milk	(optional)
1 vanilla pod	Grated nutmeg or ground cinnamon for sprinkling

Using ½oz (12g) butter, grease a 1½pt (750ml) ovenproof dish. Beat eggs and sugar together until pale and the sugar has dissolved. Heat cream or milk in a heavy saucepan with vanilla pod, bay leaf and lemon peel until it reaches boiling point. Leave to infuse for at least 30 minutes. Bring to the boil again and leave to cool a little. Pour on to egg mixture, stirring continuously. Remove lemon peel, vanilla pod and bay leaf. Stir in brandy, if using, and strain custard into prepared dish. Dot with the remaining butter and sprinkle with grated nutmeg or cinnamon.

Stand the dish in a roasting tin half-filled with water and bake in the centre of a fairly moderate oven (325°F, 160°C; Gas Mark 3) for 40–45 minutes or until firm to the touch (test with a fine skewer which should come out clean if the pudding is cooked). If necessary, place on the top shelf of the oven for a few minutes to brown the top.

Serve hot or cold with soft fruit, baked sponge pudding, fruit dumplings, baked apples or on its own. Serve with a bowl of whipped cream.

Rich Cabinet Pudding *(serves 6)* *

Also called Charter Pudding, Chancellor's Pudding, Diplomatic Pudding, Newcastle Pudding or Ratafia Pudding. It is a rich custard thickened with sponge cakes and ratafias and ornamented with glacé cherries and angelica, which dates back to the nineteenth century. Originally it would have been made with bread and butter. Cabinet Pudding is best made in a charlotte tin but a 5in (12½cm) cake tin will do.

2oz (50g) glacé cherries	4 egg yolks
1oz (25g) candied angelica	2 egg whites
¾pt (400ml) single cream or milk	1 tablespoon (1 x 15ml) sugar
½ teaspoon (½ x 5ml) grated nutmeg	½ teaspoon (½ x 5ml) vanilla essence
Grated rind of 1 lemon	4 small sponge cakes
	1oz (25g) ratafia biscuits

Butter well a charlotte or 5in (12½cm) cake tin and line the bottom with buttered greaseproof paper. Halve glacé cherries and chop angelica into diamond shapes. Scatter these over the base of the prepared tin. Heat the cream or milk with nutmeg and lemon rind until almost boiling. Whisk egg yolks, egg whites and sugar together, add cream or milk and vanilla essence, stirring well. Cut sponge cakes into small squares, crumble ratafias and put all into the prepared tin on top of the cherries and angelica. Strain eggs and milk over and leave to soak for 15 minutes. Cover with buttered greaseproof paper and tie down with string. Steam gently for about 1 hour, or until set. When cooked, allow pudding to stand for a few minutes before turning out very carefully on to a warmed serving dish and serve hot with a little Madeira, Lemon or Jam Sauce poured around the bottom of the pudding. Serve extra sauce separately.

PIES, TARTS AND FLANS

The British have as great a claim as any nation to being experts in the art of pie and tart making, and their recipes for sweet pies and tarts have hardly changed over the centuries since the Middle Ages.

The pie developed from the Roman idea of sealing meat or fish inside a flour and oil paste to cook it. This paste case or 'coffyn' was not eaten, but discarded or given to the dogs. By medieval days in northern Europe, where butter and lard were the common cooking fats, pastry began to be made, which was strong and pliable enough to be moulded into a free-standing container. Thus the 'stand' pie was invented — the ancestor of our modern 'raised' pie.

By the fifteenth century, pies had become very popular and there was an enormous variety. Most meat and fish pies included dried fruit, spices, apples, gooseberries, sugar and honey so it was not easy to tell a savoury from a sweet pie. By Elizabethan times, shorter richer pastry was being made, sometimes including butter and eggs. Pies became more and more elaborate and 'joke pies' were popular. These were enormous pies which appeared at feasts and revels filled with bran and gilded with saffron or egg yolks. After baking, the bran was removed and flocks of live birds or frogs were put into the pie which was cut open in front of the diners much to their delight and amusement — nerve-racking I should have thought.

Sweetened meat and dried fruit pies and standing pies began to go out of fashion in the Georgian period. With the increased literacy recipes began to be written down and many regional pies were recorded. Fruit tarts and pies were becoming much more adventurous and were now prepared in dishes or tins — the 'dish pye'. A large variety of fruits were put into pies and more luxurious fillings like chocolate, peaches, chestnuts and almonds made delicious pies. There was more interest in fresh fruit in place of the Tudor and Stuart 'tartstuff', a stewed fruit pulp ensuring that the fruit had been well cooked and was therefore harmless. Many of these recipes have remained more or less in their original form until the present day.

The tart and flan were developed from the 'trencher' of the Middle Ages. This was a flat disc made of a baked flour and water paste which was used as a plate. The trencher was thrown away after being used several times. Eventually, this was thought to be rather wasteful so it was made of an edible cakelike paste and called a 'tart' or 'tartlet' according to size, from the Norman-French word *tarte* or *tourte* meaning a kind of loaf.

Tarts were soon being made of short rich pastry and baked in dishes or pans. Almost anything was being put in a dish tart by the Tudor and Stuart period, and the pastry was becoming shorter and richer. Really rich butter paste was fried or baked and eaten by itself. This 'puff paste' was used for making fruit tarts and later for jam tarts, and patties. Some Elizabethan tart fillings or 'tartstuff' might seem strange to modern tastes — prunes, medlars, quinces and rosehips were stewed with sugar, red wine, cinnamon, ginger and rose-water and put into a pastry case. Flowers were also popular as tart fillings and were prepared in the spring and summer. Cowslips, violets, borage flowers, primroses, rose petals or marigold petals were beaten until small and combined with eggs and cream or curds and baked in a tart. Fruit was often set in a custard of eggs and cream.

Another interesting pastry which was introduced from France in the eighteenth century was 'crackling paste' or 'crocant' made from flour, sugar and egg whites. This was rather difficult to handle, but very rich and delicious. Usually it was baked in large circles or shapes, and sweetmeats or fruit were piled on top.

There is such an enormous variety of pies, tarts and flans, all interesting historically and good to eat, that I have found it extremely difficult to choose just a few for this book. I have tried to include some of the old favourites as well as mentioning others that might have been long forgotten. Anyway I hope you enjoy at least some of them.

English Codlin Pye *(serves 4–6)*

English apples are among the best in the world. Even the most chauvinistic of the world's *grandes cuisines* are compelled to acknowledge the quality of British-grown apples as well as English Apple Pie, which, at its traditional best, served with cream or good English Cheddar or Wensleydale cheese, must surely rank among the world's top puddings.

Pippin or codlin pyes have been very popular since Elizabethan days, flavoured with candied orange peel, saffron, cloves, cinnamon and dates. Often quinces were included to improve the flavour and rose-water was also added later. By Georgian times, fresh lemon juice and shredded lemon rind were being added to season the apples and this tradition has continued to modern times.

The apples for Tudor and Stuart fruit pies were often stewed beforehand in a brass or copper pan, when the acid of the fruit reacted with the metal, and turned the apples green! Luckily, this practice was discontinued when highly coloured foods went out of fashion.

In this recipe, the pastry is flavoured with lemon rind and the apple cores and peelings are made into a syrup to add to the pie. In the past, the poor included these with the apples in the pie to make it go further. Wild fruits, like blackberries, bilberries and elderberries were also added for the same reason.

8oz (225g) plain flour
Pinch of salt
4½oz (137g) butter
Grated rind of 1 lemon (optional)
1oz (25g) caster sugar
1 egg yolk
2 tablespoons (2 x 15ml) ice-cold
  water
2lb (900g) Bramley apples
1 quince (optional)

Juice of 1 lemon
½pt (250ml) cold water
½ teaspoon (½ x 5ml) ground
  cinnamon
2–3 cloves
2 strips lemon peel
3oz (75g) brown sugar
3oz (75g) raisins (optional)
Milk and caster sugar for glazing

Sieve flour and salt together in a mixing bowl. Rub in 4oz (125g) butter until mixture resembles fine breadcrumbs. Stir in grated lemon rind, sugar and egg yolk and enough water to mix to a firm dough. Knead until smooth and chill for 30 minutes in a floured plastic bag.

Peel, core and slice apples and peel, core and chop quince (if you have one). Put in a bowl of water with the lemon juice. Put apple and quince cores and skins into a saucepan, with water, cinnamon, cloves and lemon peel. Cover, and simmer until very soft. Remove lid and boil rapidly intil about 3 tablespoons (3 x 15ml) of syrup are left. Press through a sieve and stir in remaining butter, brown sugar and raisins.

Strain apple slices and quince pieces and layer in 1½pt (750ml) pie dish with the syrup. Roll out pastry on a lightly floured board, to make an oval 2in (5cm) wider and longer than the pie dish. Cut a strip of pastry from the edge of this oval, dampen the lip of the dish with water and put on the strip of pastry. Press firmly down. Dampen this pastry strip and put on lid of pastry, pressing down well on the edges. Flute edges and make a slit in the top of the pie to allow steam to escape, or use a pie funnel. Decorate the top with pastry leaves and brush with milk. Sprinkle with caster sugar. Bake in a fairly hot oven (400°F, 200°C; Gas Mark 6) for 20 minutes, then reduce temperature to 350°F (180°C; Gas Mark 4) for a further 20–25 minutes until the fruit is cooked and the pastry is golden brown. Remove from the oven and carefully take off the pastry lid. Add clotted or whipped cream or Custard Sauce to pie and replace pastry lid. Serve immediately with more cream or Custard Sauce, or with chunks of cheese.

Variations:
Apple and Blackcurrant Pye
Use 1½lb (675g) apples and 8oz (225g) blackcurrants. Raspberries, blackberries, damsons, plums and bilberries can also be used.

Apple and Apricot Pye
Omit lemon rind from pastry and use 8oz (225g) dried apricots and
1lb (450g) apples mixed with 2 tablespoons (2 x 15ml) apricot jam.
Brush top of pie with orange juice, or apricot jam, instead of milk, and
sprinkle with grated orange rind and caster sugar. Bake as before.

Bedfordshire Florentine Pye
Bake as before, but instead of removing pastry lid and adding cream
or Custard Sauce, make a hole in the pastry and pour mulled ale over
the apples. Make the mulled ale by heating ½pt (250ml) light ale
with 1 dessertspoon (1 x 10ml) clear honey and a pinch of nutmeg
until hot, but not boiling.

Apple and Almond Pye
Use almond pastry instead of rich shortcrust, with 8oz (225g) plain
flour, 4oz (125g) butter, 1oz (25g) caster sugar, 1oz (25g) ground
almonds and 3 tablespoons (3 x 15ml) ice-cold water.

A Florendine of Apples and Oranges *(serves 6)*
A pie of apples mixed with citrus fruits, like oranges and lemons, was
very popular in Georgian times. Originally, Seville oranges were used
and the skin from the fruit was not removed. Also called Orangeado
Pye, or Florentine Pye.

12oz (350g) plain flour	Juice of 1 orange
Pinch of salt	2oz (50g) soft brown sugar
3oz (75g) butter or margarine	1lb (450g) cooking apples
3oz (75g) lard	½ level teaspoon (½ x 5ml)
4–5 tablespoons (4–5 x 15ml)	ground cinnamon
cold water	½ level teaspoon (½ x 5ml)
¼oz (6g) softened butter	grated nutmeg
3 oranges	1 tablespoon (1 x 15ml) candied
1 lemon	orange peel or thick-cut
2 tablespoons (2 x 15ml) clear	orange marmalade
honey	Milk and caster sugar for glazing
1 tablespoon (1 x 15ml) orange	
liqueur	

Sieve flour and salt together into a mixing bowl. Rub fats into flour
until mixture resembles breadcrumbs. Add sufficient water to mix to
a firm dough. Knead lightly until smooth. Roll out half the pastry on a
lightly floured board and use to line an 8–9in (20–23cm) greased pie
dish. Brush with softened butter to prevent pastry going soggy. Peel
and thinly slice the oranges and lemon. Put honey, liqueur, orange
juice and sugar into a saucepan. Heat gently until the sugar is dissolved. Add orange and lemon slices and simmer for about 10
minutes. Peel, core and slice apples. Drain orange and lemon slices,

reserving syrup. Put fruit into pastry-lined pie dish in layers. Sprinkle each layer with spice and chopped candied peel or marmalade. Pour orange syrup over the fruit. Roll out remaining pastry to make a lid for the pie. Brush pastry with a little milk and sprinkle with caster sugar. Bake in a fairly hot oven (400°F, 200°C; Gas Mark 6) for 40–45 minutes or until pastry is golden. Serve warm or cold with whipped or pouring cream.

Variation:
Taffety Tart*
Make 2lb (900g) apples into a purée and add candied peel or marmalade, and spices. Bake a 9in (23cm) shortcrust-pastry case blind for 15 minutes. Cool and fill with apple mixture. Slice 3 oranges very thinly and arrange on top of apple filling. Bake for 20 minutes in a moderate oven (350°F, 180°C; Gas Mark 4). Serve hot or cold with whipped cream.

A Blackcurrant and Cinnamon Plate Pie *(serves 6)*
This pie, baked on a plate, is made with cinnamon-flavoured pastry. Try experimenting with various spices and different fruits.

8oz (225g) plain flour	1lb (450g) fresh or frozen
Pinch of salt	blackcurrants
1 dessertspoon (1 x 10ml) ground	4oz (125g) caster sugar
cinnamon	1/4oz (6g) softened butter
2oz (50g) butter or margarine	Milk and caster sugar for glazing
2oz (50g) lard	
About 3 tablespoons (3 x 15ml)	
cold water	

Sieve flour, salt and cinnamon together into a mixing bowl. Rub in fats until mixture resembles breadcrumbs. Add enough water to mix to a firm dough. Knead lightly until smooth, and chill.

Put blackcurrants and sugar in a saucepan. Cook over gentle heat until juices begin to run, then cook more rapidly for a few minutes, stirring frequently until the currants look thick and rich. Taste and add more sugar if necessary. Turn into a dish and cool.

Roll out pastry thinly on a lightly floured board. Using half the pastry, line a buttered 8–9in (20–23cm) ovenproof plate. Prick the bottom of the pastry with a fork, brush with softened butter (this will help to prevent pastry at the bottom from going too soggy) and chill for a few minutes. Fill the plate with cooked blackcurrants. Roll out remaining pastry to make a lid, dampening edges and pressing together well to seal. Flute edges of pie. Cut a 2in (5cm) cross in the centre of the top of the pie and fold back each triangle of pastry to make an open square showing the blackcurrants. Brush pastry with milk and sprinkle with caster sugar. Bake near the top of a hot oven (425°F, 220°C; Gas Mark 7) for 10 minutes to set the pastry and then decrease temperature to 350°F (180°C; Gas Mark 4) for a further 20–25 minutes. Serve hot or cold, sprinkled with more caster sugar and with cinnamon-flavoured whipped cream or clotted cream piled on the square of blackcurrants showing on top of the pie.

Variation:
Cranberries, raspberries, blackberries, redcurrants and bilberries all make excellent plate pies with the cinnamon pastry.

Apple Pasties *(serves 4–6)*
A pasty refers to any sweet and savoury ingredients folded and enclosed in pastry. It is the pride of the West Country, especially Cornwall. Originally the pasty was invented for the men to take to work to keep them going through the long working day, and had a savoury filling at one end and sweet at the other. This recipe just has the sweet filling and is a very popular pudding at one of our local pubs. Any flavourings and spices can be added, and try using different combinations of fruit — apple and blackberry, apple and raspberry, apricot and gooseberry. Cherry bumpers, or pasties, were traditionally eaten at the Cherry Pie Feasts of Kent and the south of England.

12oz (350g) plain flour	1 level tablespoon (1 x 15ml)
Pinch of salt	cornflour
3oz (75g) butter or margarine	2 teaspoons (2 x 5ml) lemon
3oz (75g) lard	juice
4–5 tablespoons (4–5 x 15ml)	2–3oz (50–75g) sultanas or
cold water	raisins
3–4 cooking apples	1 small egg
6–8oz (175–225g) caster or	1 tablespoon (1 x 15ml) cold
brown sugar	water
½ level teaspoon (½ x 5ml)	Sieved icing sugar for dredging
ground cinnamon	

Sieve flour and salt together into a mixing bowl. Rub in fats until the mixture resembles breadcrumbs and add sufficient water to mix into a firm dough. Knead lightly until smooth. Put in a floured plastic bag and chill for 30 minutes.

Peel, core and slice apples and put in a saucepan with the sugar and cinnamon. Combine cornflour and lemon juice together to make a paste and then add to the saucepan. Cook over low heat until apples are tender, but not broken up, stirring frequently. Remove from heat and allow to cool. Add raisins and taste for sweetness.

Roll out the pastry on a lightly floured board to about ⅛in (3mm) thickness and cut into 4 circles 8in (20cm) in diameter or 6 smaller circles. Divide the apple mixture between circles , and draw up edges of pastry to make a seam across the top, pinching edges together firmly. Crimp edges together to make a neat ridge. Place on a greased baking tray and chill again.

Beat the egg with 1 tablespoon (1 x 15ml) water. Brush glaze over pasties and make a slit in the top of each one. Bake in a hot oven (425°F, 220°C; Gas Mark 7) for 20–30 minutes or until golden brown.

Serve hot or cold with clotted or whipped cream. Try removing a small piece of pastry from the top of each pasty and putting in a dollop of clotted cream — delicious!

Richmond Maids of Honour *(makes about 18)*

Similar recipes go back to the Middle Ages, but these particular little almond-flavoured curd tarts were great favourites at the court of Henry VIII in Richmond Palace, where they were served to his many queens by the Maids of Honour. They continued and increased in popularity through the reigns of the Hanoverians. Puff pastry is traditional, but rich shortcrust or rough puff is suitable.

8oz (225g) puff pastry (bought or home-made)
About 2 tablespoons (2 x 15ml) quince or apple jelly or apricot jam
8oz (225g) curd or cottage cheese
3oz (75g) caster sugar
Grated rind of 1 lemon
2oz (50g) ground almonds
2 eggs
1 tablespoon (1 x 15ml) brandy (optional)
Icing sugar for dusting

Grease some patty or tartlet tins. Roll out pastry very thinly and using a 3¼in (8cm) cutter, cut out rounds of pastry to line tins. Spoon a little jelly or jam into the bottom of each pastry case. Chill while you prepare the filling.

Sieve curd or cottage cheese into a bowl and mix in caster sugar, lemon rind and ground almonds. Beat eggs, add brandy if using, and add to curd mixture. Mix very thoroughly until well blended. Fill each pastry case two-thirds full with cheese mixture. Bake in the centre of a fairly hot oven (400°F, 200°C; Gas Mark 6) for about 25 minutes or until well risen and puffy. Serve warm or cold, dusted with sieved icing sugar and with cream.

Variation:
Yorkshire Curd Cheesecake
Make one large tart, instead of individual ones, as before, using rich shortcrust instead of puff pastry. Omit the jelly or jam, but add 1 tablespoon (1 x 15ml) currants or raisins to the cheese mixture, leaving out 1oz (25g) caster sugar. Bake for 30–40 minutes or until filling is golden brown and puffy.

Orange-flower Cheese Tart *(serves 12)*
Cheesecakes were originally baked in a pastry case, but I prefer a
biscuit crumb base. However, do try both and see which you like.
Orange flower water was substituted for rose-water in some English
dishes towards the end of the seventeenth century. It was already
being used a great deal in France. Few English gardens had fallen
orange blossoms to make this scented water, so it was usually imported from France or Portugal. Both orange flower and rose-water
continued in popularity as food flavourings all through the eighteenth
century, but then lost favour. Recently, there has been a renewed
interest and they can be bought at any good grocer's or chemist's.
Cream cheese has been made in Britain since Roman times and a
cheesecake of a similar recipe dates back to the seventeenth century.
It is not, as some people may imagine, a modern invention from
America. Bake this the day before serving.

8oz (225g) digestive biscuits	1 level tablespoon (1 x 15ml)
8oz (225g) unsalted butter	grated orange rind
1½lb (675g) cream cheese	¼pt (150ml) soured cream
8oz (225g) caster sugar	Fresh orange slices for
3 eggs	decorating
1 teaspoon (1 x 5ml) orange	
flower water	

Put biscuits in a plastic bag and crush with a rolling pin. Melt 4oz
(125g) butter and mix together with biscuit crumbs in a mixing bowl.
Press into a 9in (23cm) spring-release cake tin to cover base. Refrigerate while making filling.

In a large mixing bowl, beat cream cheese until smooth. Slowly
beat in sugar until evenly blended. Add remaining butter, melted in a
small saucepan, beaten eggs, orange flower water and grated orange
rind. Continue beating until mixture is really smooth. Pour into
chilled crumb base. Bake in the centre of a slow oven (300°F, 150°C;
Gas Mark 2) for 45 minutes. Turn off oven, but leave cheesecake in
the oven for 30 minutes. Remove from oven and cool. Leave in a cool
place overnight if possible.

To serve, remove sides of tin and loosen cheesecake from the base
with a palette knife. Slide it on to a plate and spread the top with
soured cream. Decorate with fresh orange twists and chopped
pistachio nuts or crystallised angelica.

Variation:
Fruit Topped Cheesecake*
Make cheesecake as before but top with fresh redcurrants, raspberries, strawberries, cranberries, rhubarb, cherries, blackcurrants or
blackberries. Glaze if you wish with melted redcurrant or apple jelly.

Cherry and Brandy Dish Pie *(serves 6)*

Cherry pies and 'bumpers', or pasties, were baked and eaten at Cherry Pie Feasts to celebrate the harvesting of the fruit, in the cherry-growing areas of England, such as Kent and Buckinghamshire. In this recipe, cherry brandy is added to the pie after baking, but it is just as good without. Any fruit can be used instead of cherries — gooseberries, plums, damsons, apricots, greengages and rhubarb.

8oz (225g) plain flour
Pinch of salt
4½oz (137g) butter
5oz (150g) caster sugar
1 egg yolk
2 tablespoons (2 x 15ml) ice-cold
   water

2lb (900g) stoned cherries
Milk and caster sugar for glazing
2 tablespoons (2 x 15ml) cherry
   brandy or brandy
3 tablespoons (3 x 15ml) double
   cream

Sieve flour and salt together into a mixing bowl. Rub in 4oz (125g) butter until mixture resembles breadcrumbs. Stir in 1oz (25g) caster sugar, egg yolk and enough cold water to mix to a firm dough. Knead lightly until smooth, put into a floured plastic bag and chill for at least 30 minutes.

Fill a 1½pt (750ml) pie dish with stoned cherries, sprinkle with extra sugar and dot with remaining butter.

Roll out pastry on a lightly floured board and cover dish of cherries. Flute edges of pastry lid and make a couple of slits in the top to let out the steam. Decorate with pastry trimmings. Brush with milk and caster sugar. Bake in the centre of a moderately hot oven (400°F, 200°C; Gas Mark 6) for 20 minutes, then reduce heat to 375°F (190°C; Gas Mark 5) and continue cooking for 20–25 minutes or until pastry is golden brown.

Remove from oven and cut neatly round the lid of the pie. Lift off carefully, and pour cherry brandy and cream over the fruit. Replace pastry lid, dredge with extra caster sugar and return to the oven for 5 minutes. Serve hot with whipped or clotted cream.

Variation:
Summer Fruit and Brandy Pie
Use a combination of soft summer fruits instead of cherries — 1lb
(450g) raspberries with 8oz (225g) blackcurrants and 8oz (225g) redcurrants. Use brandy instead of cherry brandy.

Rich Chocolate Pye *(serves 6)* *

Chocolate was introduced into Britain in the mid-seventeenth
century from Mexico where the Aztecs had mixed it with honey. It
remained a luxury drink as long as the price of sugar was high, and
was never as popular as coffee or tea. A pie with a chocolate filling like
this one would have been considered a great luxury and in fact still is.

10oz (275g) plain flour
Pinch of salt
5½oz (165g) butter
5oz (150g) caster sugar
4 egg yolks
About 2 tablespoons (2 x 15ml)
   ice-cold water
Pinch of ground nutmeg
¼ level teaspoon (¼ x 5ml) salt

4oz (125g) caster or soft brown
   sugar
¾pt (400ml) milk
4oz (125g) plain chocolate
1 teaspoon (1 x 5ml) vanilla
   essence
2 egg whites
1oz (25g) toasted flaked almonds
   for decorating
Crystallised violets or rose petals

Sieve 8oz (225g) flour and pinch of salt together. Rub in 4oz (125g)
butter until mixture resembles breadcrumbs. Stir in 1oz (25g) sugar.
Beat 1 egg yolk with a little of the water and add to dry ingredients
with sufficient extra water to mix to a firm dough. Knead lightly until
smooth, put into a floured plastic bag and chill for at least 30 minutes.
   Roll out pastry and line a 9in (23cm) flan ring and bake blind at
400°F (200°C; Gas Mark 6) for 10–15 minutes. Remove foil or baking
beans and bake for another 5 minutes. Remove from oven and leave to
cool.
   Sieve remaining flour, nutmeg and ¼ level teaspoon (¼ x 5ml) salt
together into a saucepan. Stir in the 4oz (125g) caster or soft brown
sugar and milk. Break chocolate into small pieces and add to saucepan. Heat until chocolate is melted, stirring continuously. Whisk
until chocolate and milk are blended, then increase heat and cook for
about 10 minutes, stirring all the time. Remove saucepan from heat.
Beat remaining 3 egg yolks and whisk in a small amount of hot chocolate mixture. Slowly, pour egg mixture into the saucepan, stirring
rapidly. Cook over low heat, stirring until mixture is very thick and
creamy, but do not boil. Remove from heat and stir in remaining
butter and vanilla essence. Pour into cooled pastry case.
   Whisk egg whites until stiff, but not dry. Whisk in 2oz (50g) caster
sugar until thick and glossy. Carefully fold in remaining 2oz (50g)

caster sugar with a metal spoon. Pile on top of the chocolate pie. Bake in a moderately hot oven (400°F, 200°C; Gas Mark 6) for 10 minutes until crisp and lightly browned. Chill before serving. Decorate with toasted flaked almonds and crystallised violets or rose petals.

Cumberland Rum Nicky *(serves 6)*

Small versions of this pie, similar to mince pies and called Rum Nickies, can also be made. It recalls the days in the eighteenth century when Whitehaven in Cumbria was one of the leading ports in the rum trade with the West Indies.

8oz (225g) plain flour	4oz (125g) chopped dates
Pinch of salt	2oz (50g) chopped preserved
4oz (125g) unsalted butter	ginger
2oz (50g) caster sugar	2oz (50g) butter
1 egg yolk	2 tablespoons (2 x 15ml) dark
2–3 tablespoons (2–3 x 15ml)	rum
ice-cold water	Icing sugar for dredging

Sieve flour and salt together into a mixing bowl. Rub in butter until mixture resembles breadcrumbs. Stir in half the sugar. Add egg yolk and enough very cold water to mix to a firm dough. Knead lightly until smooth. Put dough in a floured plastic bag and chill for at least 30 minutes.

Roll out pastry on a lightly floured board. Line a greased 8in (20cm) pie or ovenproof plate with half the pastry. Sprinkle over chopped dates and ginger. Cream butter and remaining sugar together until pale and fluffy. Beat in rum gradually. Spread mixture over fruit in pie plate. Cover with remaining pastry, sealing edges well. Make a couple of slits in the top of the pastry, flute edges and decorate as you wish with pastry trimmings. Bake in the centre of a moderately hot oven (400°F, 200°C; Gas Mark 6) for 10–15 minutes and then reduce temperature to 350°F (180°C; Gas Mark 4) for a further 25–30 minutes. Serve hot, dredged with icing sugar and with whipped or clotted cream or Rum and Orange Butter.

Royal Pye *(serves 6–8)*
In Elizabethan times a 'royal' pye was any savoury or sweet pie which
was 'iced' with sugar and egg white. This original glaze was more like
our modern 'royal icing' rather than our modern meringue which is
obviously a descendant. Try coating a fruit pie with royal icing just
before it is cooked and then continue cooking in the oven for a further
ten minutes. It is particularly good with a sharp fruit filling such as
rhubarb or damson.

This particular Royal Pye is filled with mincemeat, apples and
grapes and is ideal for serving at Christmas alongside the plum
pudding. The pie is made of rich shortcrust pastry which was originally called 'biscuit crust pastry'.

8oz (225g) plain flour	1lb (450g) Cox's eating apples
Pinch of salt	4oz (125g) green grapes
4oz (125g) unsalted butter	1lb (450g) home-made
5oz (150g) caster sugar	mincemeat
1 small egg	1–2 tablespoons (1–2 x 15ml)
About 2 tablespoons (2 x 15ml)	brandy or sherry
ice-cold water	2 egg whites

Sieve flour and salt together into a mixing bowl. Cut butter into flour
until well coated and in small pieces. Rub in with fingertips until
mixture resembles fine breadcrumbs. Stir in 1oz (25g) sugar and
beaten egg and enough cold water to mix to a firm dough. Knead
pastry lightly on a floured board until smooth. Chill for 30 minutes.

Peel, core and chop apples. Peel and pip grapes and cut in half if
very large. Mix with mincemeat. Moisten with brandy or sherry. Roll
pastry out on a lightly floured board and line a 9in (23cm) flan tin.
Chill again for about 15 minutes while the oven is warming. Set oven
at 375°F (190°C; Gas Mark 5) and put in a baking tray to heat (this
will help to cook the bottom of your pastry).

Fill pastry case with the mincemeat mixture and place on a baking
sheet in pre-heated oven. Bake for 30 minutes.

Whisk egg whites until stiff and whisk in 2oz (50g) caster sugar
until smooth and glossy. Gently fold in remaining sugar and pile
meringue on top of cooked mincemeat pie. Put back in the oven and
bake for a further 15–20 minutes until meringue is crisp and lightly
brown. Serve hot with whipped cream flavoured with a little brandy
or sherry.

Variation:
Almond Royal Pye
Use almond pastry instead of a rich shortcrust — 8oz (225g) plain
flour, 4oz (125g) butter, 1oz (25g) caster sugar, 1oz (25g) ground
almonds and 3 tablespoons (3 x 15ml) ice-cold water.

Pilgrim Pye *(serves 6–8)*

This is the pumpkin pie that the Pilgrim Fathers took to America with them, where it became a national dish. Pumpkin pies were much enjoyed in Tudor times alongside other vegetables pies such as carrot and parsnip which had a natural sweetness. The vegetables were sliced and fried with sweet herbs and spices, and enriched with eggs and dried fruit. Pumpkin pie went out of fashion during the eighteenth century and has never regained its former popularity, except perhaps at a Hallowe'en feast.

8oz (225g) plain flour
Pinch of salt
4oz (125g) butter
1oz (25g) caster sugar
Grated rind of 2 lemons
1 egg yolk
2–3 tablespoons (2–3 x 15ml)
  ice-cold water
1lb (450g) pumpkin flesh
Pinch of salt
4oz (125g) soft brown sugar
¾ teaspoon (¾ x 5ml) ground
  ginger
½ teaspoon (½ x 5ml) ground
  cinnamon

¼ teaspoon (¼ x 5ml) ground
  nutmeg
1 tablespoon (1 x 15ml) thick
  honey
Grated rind of 1 orange
2 eggs
¼pt (150ml) double cream
1 teaspoon (1 x 5ml) syrup from
  preserved stem ginger or
  caster sugar
2oz (50g) toasted chopped
  walnuts

Sieve flour and salt together into a mixing bowl. Rub butter with fingertips into flour until mixture resembles fine breadcrumbs. Stir in the sugar and half the lemon rind. Beat egg yolk with sufficient cold water to bind mixture together and make a firm dough. Knead lightly until smooth. Chill for at least 30 minutes in a floured plastic bag.

Cut up pumpkin flesh, removing any seeds. Heat gently until tender — about 15 minutes. Strain and mash to a pulp. Put in a mixing bowl and add salt, brown sugar, ½ teaspoon (½ x 5ml) ginger, other spices, honey, orange and remaining lemon rind. Leave to cool.

Roll out pastry on a lightly floured board and line a deep greased 8 or 9in (20 or 23cm) pie plate. Beat eggs and add to pumpkin mixture. Pour into prepared pastry case and bake in the centre of a moderate oven (375°F, 190°C; Gas Mark 5) for 45–55 minutes or until filling is set. (Test with a skewer — it should come out clean.) Remove from the oven and leave to cool.

Whip cream until it stands in soft peaks. Sweeten with ginger syrup or sugar and sprinkle with remaining ground ginger. Just before serving, cover pumpkin pie with cream and sprinkle with chopped toasted walnuts.

A Tartys of Raspberries and Cream *(serves 6–8)* *
This delicious tart recipe is based on one which dates back to the
seventeenth century. In the original, the raspberries were highly
spiced and cooked in a thin-lidded puff-pastry pie. It was later, in the
eighteenth century, that there was a decline in the use of spices. Here,
the fruit filling is set in an egg custard which was a very popular way of
making a fruit pie.

Raspberries were first recorded as a garden fruit in Britain in 1548.
Many other fruits can be used in place of the raspberries — try strawberries, cherries or rhubarb.

8oz (225g) plain flour	2lb (900g) fresh or frozen
Pinch of salt	raspberries
4oz (125g) unsalted butter	3 eggs
7oz (200g) caster sugar	1 level tablespoon (1 x 15ml)
1 egg yolk	cornflour
2 tablespoons (2 x 15ml) ice-cold	½pt (250ml) single cream
water	1 tablespoon (1 x 15ml) Kirsch or
2–3 drops vanilla essence	Framboise (optional)

Sieve flour and salt together into a mixing bowl. Cut butter into the
flour until well coated and in small pieces. Rub in with fingertips until
mixture resembles fine breadcrumbs. Stir in 1oz (25g) caster sugar.
Mix the egg yolk with the cold water and vanilla essence and stir into
flour mixture. Mix to a firm dough adding more water if necessary.
Knead lightly until smooth and chill in refrigerator for 30 minutes.

Roll out on a lightly floured board and line a 10in (25cm) flan tin.
Chill again and then bake blind in a fairly hot oven (400°F, 200°C;
Gas Mark 6) for 10–15 minutes. Remove from the oven and take out
foil or baking beans and return to the oven for a further 5 minutes.

Cool the pastry and then fill with raspberries. Sprinkle with 4oz
(125g) caster sugar. Beat eggs, remaining sugar and cornflour
together until almost white. Stir in cream and liqueur, if using. Pour
over raspberries and bake in the centre of a moderate oven (350°F,
180°C; Gas Mark 4) for 35–40 minutes or until the custard is set.

Serve hot or warm, sprinkled with caster sugar and with whipped
cream.

Variations:
*Almond Raspberry Cream Tart**
Instead of rich shortcrust, use almond pastry — 8oz (225g) plain
flour, 4oz (125g) butter, 1oz (25g) caster sugar, 1oz (25g) ground
almonds and 3 tablespoons (3 x 15ml) cold water.

A Tartys of Pears and Ginger
Use 4 firm dessert pears cut in halves and 2oz (50g) chopped preserved stem ginger. Continue as before.

A Sweet Egg Pie *(serves 4–6)* *

Also known as Custard Tart and Transparent Pudding, this pie has been popular since Elizabethan days when the filling was made with vegetables or fruit, eggs, thick cream and lots of spices. Originally the pastry case was literally to provide a 'coffyn' or container in which to cook the custard.

6oz (175g) plain flour	½ level teaspoon (½ x 5ml)
3oz (75g) unsalted butter	cornflour
2oz (50g) caster sugar	½pt (250ml) single cream or
1 egg yolk	milk
1–2 tablespoons (1–2 x 15ml)	1 vanilla pod
ice-cold water	Grated nutmeg or cinnamon for
3 eggs	sprinkling

Sieve flour into a mixing bowl. Rub the butter into the flour using fingertips. Stir in ½oz (12g) sugar. Beat the egg yolk with cold water and add to flour and butter mixture. Collect into a dough, knead very lightly and set aside in a cool place to chill for 30 minutes. Then roll out on a lightly floured board and line an 8in (20cm) flan tin. Chill again. Bake blind in a fairly hot oven (375°F, 190°C; Gas Mark 5) for 15–20 minutes until pastry is almost cooked. Remove from oven, empty, and leave to cool while you make the filling. Lower oven to 300°F (150°C; Gas Mark 2).

Beat eggs and mix in cornflour and remaining sugar. Beat until sugar granules have dissolved. Heat cream or milk with pierced vanilla pod until it reaches boiling point. Pour on to egg mixture, whisking continuously. Remove vanilla pod. Strain through a sieve into flan case and sprinkle with grated nutmeg or ground cinnamon. Bake in the centre of a cool oven (300°F, 150°C; Gas Mark 2) for about 30 minutes or until custard is set (test with a fine skewer which should come out clean). Remove from oven when set and leave to cool a little before removing from flan tin. Serve warm or cold, decorated with a few fresh flowers.

Treacle Tart *(serves 6–8)*

With the setting up of sugar refineries in British ports in the late eighteenth century, treacle, the syrup remaining after the sugar had been refined, was generally available. One of its first uses was to make gingerbread which was extremely popular at fairs and feast-days. This may have been the origin of Treacle Tart, because the old medieval gingerbread was made by pressing breadcrumbs, treacle, spices and colourings together — very different from our modern spongy ginger cake. By the late eighteenth century, treacle was being replaced in tarts by golden syrup, but the name remained. In the north it continued to be popular as it was a cheaper sweetener.

8oz (225g) plain flour
Pinch of salt
2oz (50g) butter or margarine
2oz (50g) lard
About 3 tablespoons (3 x 15ml)
cold water
9 rounded tablespoons (9 x 15ml)
golden syrup
Grated rind of 1 lemon

1 tablespoon (1 x 15ml) lemon
juice (optional)
9 heaped tablespoons (9 x 15ml)
fresh white breadcrumbs
1 teaspoon (1 x 5ml) ground
ginger
1 egg beaten with 1 teaspoon
(1 x 5ml) water

Sieve flour and salt together into a mixing bowl. Cut fats into small pieces and place in the flour. Rub fat lightly into flour with cool finger-tips, until mixture resembles fine breadcrumbs. Add enough cold water gradually and mix with a palette knife until mixture forms a soft dough. Put in a floured plastic bag and chill for 30 minutes before using.

Roll out two-thirds of the pastry on a floured board and line a 10in (25cm) shallow pie plate or flan tin. Warm syrup, lemon rind and lemon juice, if you are using, over gentle heat. Stir in breadcrumbs and ginger. Pour into pastry case. Roll out remaining pastry, cut into strips and make a lattice pattern with them over the top of the tart, either twisted or plain. Crimp the edge of the tart with a fork, pressing lattice strips down firmly. Brush with beaten egg and water.

Bake in the centre of a moderate oven (375°F, 190°C; Gas Mark 5) for 25–30 minutes or until pastry is crisp and golden brown. Serve warm with clotted cream, or Honey and Brandy Iced Cream.

Rhubarb and Orange Lattice Tart *(serves 6)*

This traditional tart is made with cinnamon- or ginger-flavoured pastry and filled with rhubarb, flavoured with orange. The lattice top is a very traditional way of finishing off a pie — not for decoration but for marking. In the past, the housewife would make a large number of both savoury and sweet pies and bake them all at the same time, either in her own oven or in the village baker's oven, and of course the pies all had to be identified with either lattices, slits, or marks of some description.

7oz (200g) plain flour
Pinch of salt
1 teaspoon (1 x 5ml) ground
cinnamon or ground ginger
3oz (75g) butter
1oz (25g) caster sugar
2 eggs
2 tablespoons (2 x 15ml) ice-cold
water

1/4oz (6g) softened butter
1lb (450g) rhubarb
8oz (225g) white or brown sugar
Grated rind of 1 orange
4 tablespoons (4 x 15ml) orange
juice
Milk and caster sugar for
glazing

Sieve 6oz (175g) flour, salt and ground cinnamon or ginger together into a mixing bowl. Rub in butter lightly until mixture resembles breadcrumbs. Stir in caster sugar and mix to a firm dough with 1 beaten egg and the water. Roll out the pastry on a lightly floured board and line an 8in (20cm) greased flan tin or pie plate. Brush with softened butter to prevent the pastry at the bottom going soggy. Chill for 30 minutes.

Cut rhubarb into short even lengths. Arrange in the pastry case. Put remaining flour, sugar and orange rind in a small basin. Add beaten egg and blend well until smooth. Heat the orange juice in a small saucepan until it reaches boiling point. Pour on to egg mixture gradually, stirring continuously. Return to pan and bring to the boil again, stirring all the time. Pour over rhubarb.

Roll pastry trimmings into long strips ½in (1cm) wide and arrange in a lattice pattern over the top of the tart, twisting them like barley sugar, and sticking the ends down with a little water. Brush each strip with a little milk and sprinkle with sugar. Bake in a hot oven (425°F, 220°C; Gas Mark 7) for 35–40 minutes or until pastry is golden brown.

Serve hot or cold with whipped or clotted cream or Custard Sauce.

Walnut and Honey Tart *(serves 6–8)*

Walnuts have been grown in Britain for centuries and in the past were used in cooking far more than they are nowadays. Villagers used to gather them in the autumn and make them into pies, puddings, sauces, cakes, soups and stuffings. They were also added to meat and fish dishes, and pickled. This tart is very, very rich, so a little goes a long way.

6oz (175g) plain flour	5oz (150g) soft brown sugar
Pinch of salt	Grated rind of 1 orange
1½oz (40g) margarine or butter	3 eggs
1½oz (40g) lard	6oz (175g) clear honey
About 2 tabespoons (2 x 15ml) cold water	½ teaspoon (½ x 5ml) vanilla essence
3oz (75g) butter	4oz (125g) walnut halves

Sieve flour and salt together into a mixing bowl. Rub in fats until mixture resembles fine breadcrumbs. Add enough water to mix to a firm dough. Knead lightly until smooth and chill for at least 30 minutes.

Roll out pastry thinly on a lightly floured board and line an 8in (20cm) flan tin or ovenproof dish. Bake blind in a fairly hot oven (400°F, 200°C; Gas Mark 6) for 5–7 minutes, remove from the oven and take out foil or beans. Replace in the oven and cook for a further 5 minutes. Set aside to cool.

Cream the butter, gradually adding sugar and orange rind. Beat until well blended. Beat eggs and add gradually to creamed mixture, beating continuously. Add honey and vanilla essence, mixing to a smooth consistency. Sprinkle walnut halves in the bottom of the prepared pastry case. Pour over honey mixture and bake in the centre of a moderately hot oven (400°F, 200°C; Gas Mark 6) for 40–45 minutes or until set. Make sure it doesn't brown too quickly — protect top and pastry edges with foil if necessary.

Serve cold with plenty of chilled whipped or clotted cream.

A Lady's Tart *(serves 6)*
This nineteenth-century tart was originally filled with apricot preserve and decorated with flaked almonds. It had a decorative edge of small pastry circles. In this recipe, I have used four varieties of jam laid in sections and divided by strips of pastry. This colourful jam tart used to be the pride of housewives, who, of course, used their best home-made jams.

8oz (225g) plain flour
Pinch of salt
2oz (50g) butter or margarine
2oz (50g) lard
3 tablespoons (3 x 15ml) cold water
2 tablespoons (2 x 15ml) apricot jam
2 tablespoons (2 x 15ml) strawberry or raspberry jam

2 tablespoons (2 x 15ml) green gooseberry jam
2 tablespoons (2 x 15ml) blackcurrant jam
Milk or water for brushing

To glaze:
1 egg
1 tablespoon (1 x 15ml) cold water

Sieve flour and salt together into a mixing bowl. Rub in fats until mixture resembles fine breadcrumbs. Stir in enough water to give a firm dough. Knead lightly until smooth and chill in a floured polythene bag for at least 30 minutes.

Roll out pastry thinly on a lightly floured board, and using two-thirds of the pastry line a greased 10in (25cm) pie or ovenproof plate. Divide pastry base into 8 sections, marking with a knife. Spread each section with the different jams alternating the colours. Cut pastry trimmings into narrow strips and arrange in twists across the tart dividing the jams. Cut remaining pastry into small circles with a 1in (2½cm) cutter. Brush rim of pastry-lined plate with a little milk or water and arrange circles around the edge overlapping them a little.

Beat the egg with the water and brush pastry circles and twists carefully to glaze. Bake in the centre of a moderate oven (375°F, 190°C; Gas Mark 5) for about 30 minutes or until pastry is golden brown. Serve hot or cold with Custard Sauce or with whipped or clotted cream.

97

STEAMED AND BOILED PUDDINGS

The ancestor of the boiled pudding was the medieval 'pottage', a kind of porridge of cereal, honey, wild fruits and shredded meat or fish. Later, in Tudor and Stuart days, meatless puddings of breadcrumbs, rice or oatmeal were mixed with milk, cream, eggs, spices and dried fruit, stuffed into animal guts and boiled. They were then removed from the guts and browned in front of the fire, and served sprinkled with sugar and melted butter. Although animal guts were useful as containers for boiling puddings, they had several disadvantages, because they were awkward to clean, inconvenient to fill and of course were only available at pig- or sheep-killing time. Experiments were made using other containers such as hollowed turnips, carrots and cucumbers. This practice continued all through the seventeenth and eighteenth centuries, but did not lead to any real development in pudding making.

The future of the boiled suet pudding as one of England's national dishes was assured only when the pudding cloth came into use. It received one of its earliest mentions in a recipe dated 1617 for College Pudding or Cambridge Pudding. The invention of the pudding cloth or bag firmly cut the link between puddings and animal guts. Puddings could now be made at any time and they became a regular part of the daily fare of almost all classes.

One of the advantages of a pudding wrapped in its pudding cloth was that it could be simmered along with the meat by the poorer housewife, whose principal means of cooking in the seventeenth century was still a cauldron suspended from a pot-hook over the fire.

Suet was sometimes replaced by bone marrow in boiled puddings. Ground almonds were often an ingredient and dried fruit was added liberally in some recipes to make a 'plum' pudding. It was found that dried fruit did not lose its flavour and consistency as much as fresh fruit, although before the end of the seventeenth century the boiled pudding composed of a suet crust wrapped around a filling of apples or gooseberries was in existence. Mace, nutmeg, cinnamon and ginger were spices commonly used for seasoning.

Heavy suet boiled puddings reached their peak of popularity in Victorian times when they were much loved by Prince Albert. He was responsible for introducing the 'plum pudding' as part of traditional Christmas fare.

Nowadays, we usually steam puddings in a pudding basin rather than boiling them in a cloth to get a lighter result. If you want to try the traditional method, make sure that your pudding cloth is dry and clean, well buttered and floured. The pudding mixture should be tied loosely in the cloth to allow for expansion and the water must always be boiling before the pudding is lowered into the saucepan. Also, the pudding must be moved about during cooking to prevent it from sticking to the bottom of the saucepan. When the pudding is cooked, remove it from the boiling water and dip it into a pan of cold water for a few seconds. This will prevent it from sticking to the pudding cloth.

To steam a pudding, use a steamer, or place the pudding in a saucepan with gently boiling water coming halfway up the basin. Do not allow the water to go off the boil and top up as necessary with boiling water. If you stand your pudding basin on a trivet or saucer in the saucepan, any jam, marmalade or syrup at the bottom of the pudding will not caramelise.

Apple Hat *(serves 6)*

8oz (225g) self-raising flour	3 cloves
Pinch of salt	Pinch of ground cinnamon
4oz (125g) shredded suet	Pinch of ground ginger
6–8 tablespoons (6–8 x 15ml)	Grated rind and juice of
cold water	½ lemon or 1 orange
1½lb (675g) cooking apples	2oz (50g) unsalted butter
2oz (50g) raisins or sultanas	1 tablespoon (1 x 15ml) clotted
3oz (75g) brown or white sugar	cream

Butter well a 2pt (1 litre) pudding basin.

Sieve flour with salt into a mixing bowl. Stir in suet and mix with sufficient cold water to make a soft, light dough. Knead lightly and roll out on a floured board about ¼in (6mm) thick. Use two-thirds of the pastry to line prepared basin.

Peel, core and slice apples and fill lined basin with layers of apples, raisins or sultanas, sugar and spices. Add lemon or orange rind and juice and the butter, cut into small pieces. Cover basin with reserved piece of pastry, dampening edges and pressing together firmly. Cover with a piece of pleated well-buttered greaseproof paper followed by a piece of buttered foil with a pleat in the centre, at right angles to the greaseproof paper to allow room for the pudding to rise. Tie down securely with string. Steam for 2–2½ hours, topping up with boiling water as necessary.

Turn out on to a warmed serving plate and remove a square of the pastry from the top of the pudding. Pop in a tablespoon of clotted cream which will melt into the pudding! Serve hot with more cream and brown sugar or with Custard Sauce.

Variations:
Apple and Bramble Hat
Use 1lb (450g) cooking apples and 8oz (225g) blackberries. Omit raisins.

Apple and Marmalade Hat
Replace grated rind and juice of lemon with 1–2 tablespoons (1–2 x 15ml) orange or quince marmalade, and omit raisins. Serve with Marmalade Sauce.

Apple and Golden Syrup Hat
Use 3 tablespoons (3 x 15ml) golden syrup instead of brown sugar to make a sweeter, richer pudding. Serve with Syrup Sauce.

Apple and Gin Hat
Make as for Apple Hat but pour a dessertspoon (1 x 10ml) gin over each serving!

Rich Chocolate and Walnut Pudding *(serves 6)*

3oz (75g) plain chocolate,
   e.g. Menier or Bournville
2oz (50g) butter
½pt (250ml) milk
2oz (50g) caster sugar
2 eggs, separated

½ teaspoon (½ x 5ml) vanilla
   essence
5oz (150g) fresh white
   breadcrumbs
3oz (75g) finely chopped
   walnuts

Well butter a 1½pt (750ml) pudding basin. Melt chocolate and butter in a basin over a saucepan of hot water. (Don't be tempted to use cooking chocolate for this pudding — the flavour will not be as good.) Remove chocolate from heat and stir. Warm milk in a saucepan and add gradually to chocolate mixture. Stir in the sugar. Beat egg yolks and add vanilla essence. Stir into chocolate mixture. Add breadcrumbs and walnuts. Whisk egg whites until stiff and fold gently into pudding mixture. Turn into prepared basin and cover with buttered kitchen foil, making a pleat across the top to allow pudding to rise. Tie securely with string. Steam for 1½–2 hours until well risen and springy.

Turn out on to a warmed serving plate and serve either hot with Chocolate Sauce or pouring cream, or cold with whipped cream.

Variations:
Rich Chocolate Pudding
Omit finely chopped walnuts.

Rich Chocolate and Orange Pudding
Add grated rind of 1 orange and ½ lemon and 1 tablespoon (1 x 15ml) brandy.

A Bachelor's Pudding *(serves 6)*

2 tablespoons (2 x 15ml) golden syrup	2 tablespoons (2 x 15ml) milk or water
4oz (125g) unsalted butter	1lb (450g) cooking apples
4oz (125g) caster sugar	2oz (50g) currants
2 eggs	3oz (75g) demerara sugar
5oz (150g) self-raising flour	1 level teaspoon (1 x 5ml) ground cinnamon

Butter a 2pt (1 litre) pudding basin well. Pour golden syrup into the bottom. Cream butter and sugar together until pale and fluffy. Beat eggs and add gradually to creamed mixture. Fold in flour gently with a metal spoon. Add sufficient milk or water to make a soft dropping consistency. Peel, core and slice apples and mix with currants, sugar and cinnamon. Pour a layer of pudding mixture into the bottom of the prepared basin, top with a layer of apple mixture and then another layer of pudding mixture and then remaining apples. Spoon over remaining pudding. Cover with buttered kitchen foil, making a pleat across the centre to allow pudding to rise. Steam for 2–2½ hours until firm and well risen. Turn out on to a warmed serving dish and serve with clotted cream or Custard Sauce.

Brigade Pudding *(serves 6)*
This is a pudding popular in the north of England, consisting of layers of suet pastry with mincemeat between each layer. In fact I first tasted it in Yorkshire cooked by my sister.

8oz (225g) self-raising flour	6–8 tablespoons (6–8 x 15ml) cold water
¼ teaspoon (¼ x 5ml) salt	2 tablespoons (2 x 15ml) golden syrup
4oz (125g) shredded suet	8oz (225g) mincemeat
Grated rind of ½ lemon	

Butter well a 2pt (1 litre) pudding basin. Sieve flour and salt together into a mixing bowl, and stir in suet and lemon rind. Add sufficient water to mix to a soft but not sticky dough. Turn on to a floured board and divide into 4 portions, each a little larger than the next. Spoon golden syrup into the bottom of prepared basin. Pat smallest portion of dough into a circle large enough to fit bottom of basin. Spread over a layer of mincemeat, then make another circle of dough to fit the basin. Continue in layers, ending with a top layer of dough. Cover with buttered kitchen foil with a good pleat across the centre to allow pudding to rise. Tie down securely with string. Steam for 2½–3 hours, topping up with boiling water as necessary.
   Turn out on to a warmed serving plate and serve very hot with Custard or Lemon Sauce.

College Pudding *(serves 6)*

Also called Cambridge Pudding and reputed to have been the first pudding boiled in a cloth rather than in animal guts or a vegetable container. It was served to students at Cambridge University in 1617. Nowadays, it is easier to cook this pudding in a basin. It should be dark and spicy.

3oz (75g) self-raising flour	3oz (75g) raisins
3oz (75g) fresh white or brown	2oz (50g) currants
breadcrumbs	1oz (25g) chopped candied peel
1 teaspoon (1 x 5ml) mixed spice	2oz (50g) brown sugar
3oz (75g) shredded suet	1 egg
Pinch of salt	6 tablespoons (6 x 15ml) milk

Well butter a 2pt (1 litre) pudding basin. Mix together all dry ingredients in a bowl. Beat egg and add to dry ingredients with enough milk to produce a soft dropping consistency.

Spoon into prepared basin, cover with buttered kitchen foil, making a pleat across the centre to allow the pudding to rise. Tie foil firmly in place with string, making a handle across the top so that you can lift the pudding easily. Steam for 2–2½ hours, topping up with boiling water when necessary.

Remove from heat and allow to shrink slightly before turning out on to a warmed serving plate. Serve very hot with Custard, Lemon or a Hard Sauce.

Canary Pudding *(serves 6)*

This is one of the basic English light steamed puddings. In the past it would have been made of suet and boiled for at least three hours. Later, it was adapted and given a spongy texture which is much lighter and easier on the stomach! It can be cooked in individual small moulds or darioles and called Castle Puddings or Sutherland Puddings. It was called Canary Pudding, because originally it was made with a flavouring of Madeira, the sweet sherry-like fortified wine from the Canary Islands. Experiment with different flavourings — coffee, lemon, orange and vanilla.

4oz (125g) unsalted butter	2oz (50g) fresh white
4oz (125g) caster sugar	breadcrumbs
2 eggs	Grated rind of 1 lemon
2oz (50g) self-raising flour	1–2 tablespoons (1–2 x 15ml)
	Madeira or sweet sherry

Well butter a 2pt (1 litre) pudding basin. Cream butter and sugar together until pale and fluffy. Beat eggs and add gradually to creamed mixture, beating well between each addition. Sieve flour and gently fold into pudding mixture. Carefully stir in breadcrumbs and lemon rind and mix to a soft dropping consistency with Madeira or sherry. Spoon into prepared basin, cover with buttered kitchen foil, making a pleat across centre. (This pudding needs room to rise to ensure that it is very light.) Tie down firmly with string and steam for 2–2½ hours or until well risen and spongy, topping up with more boiling water as necessary.

When cooked, turn out carefully on to a warmed serving plate and serve hot with hot Lemon, Madeira or Butterscotch Sauce.

Variation:
Black Cap Canary Pudding
Put 3 tablespoons (3 x 15ml) blackcurrant jam in the bottom of the basin before filling with pudding mixture.

The Duchess's Pudding *(serves 6)*
A light steamed almond-flavoured sponge pudding with chopped nuts, peel and dried fruit. I don't know which duchess inspired this pudding, but it is delicious!

4oz (125g) unsalted butter	1oz (25g) chopped candied peel
4oz (125g) caster sugar	1oz (25g) chopped walnuts or
2 eggs	almonds
5oz (150g) self-raising flour	A few drops of almond essence
1oz (25g) raisins	About 2 tablespoons (2 x 15ml)
1oz (25g) chopped glacé cherries	water or milk

Butter well a 1½pt (750ml) pudding basin. Cream butter and sugar together until pale and fluffy. Beat eggs and add gradually to creamed mixture beating well between each addition. Sieve flour and fold gently into mixture using a metal spoon. Add fruit, peel and nuts, almond essence and enough water or milk to give a soft dropping consistency. Put into prepared basin, cover with buttered kitchen foil, making a pleat across the centre to allow pudding to rise, and tie down securely with string. Steam for 1½–2 hours over rapidly boiling water, until firm and well risen. When cooked, turn pudding on to a warmed serving plate and serve hot with Apricot, Jam, Lemon or Custard Sauce.

Rich Fig and Almond Pudding *(serves 6)*

Fig Pudding was traditionally eaten on Mothering Sunday in Lancashire. Further south in Buckinghamshire and the home counties, figs were eaten on Palm Sunday. This custom was said to be connected with the Gospel account of the barren fig tree.

8oz (225g) dried figs	6oz (175g) fresh white
8oz (225g) dates	breadcrumbs
4oz (125g) raisins	6oz (175g) shredded suet
2 tablespoons (2 x 15ml) brandy,	2oz (50g) ground almonds
rum, or Madeira	3 eggs
8oz (225g) self-raising flour	Grated rind and juice of 1 lemon
Pinch of salt	A little milk or water

Chop figs and dates, mix with raisins and sprinkle with brandy. Cover and leave to soak for at least 1 hour. Butter well a 2pt (1 litre) pudding basin. Sieve flour and salt together into a mixing bowl. Stir in crumbs, suet and ground almonds. Beat eggs and mix into dry ingredients with lemon rind and juice. Add fruit and mix thoroughly, adding a little milk or water if necessary, to make a soft dropping consistency. Turn into prepared basin, cover with buttered kitchen foil making a pleat across the centre to allow the pudding room to rise. Tie down securely with string. Steam for 4 hours until firm and well risen. Turn out on to a warm serving plate and serve hot with a Hard Sauce or Madeira Sauce, or with clotted cream.

A Golden Pudding *(serves 6)*

This lovely syrupy sponge pudding with a golden coating of syrup — hence its name — has been popular country-wide since golden syrup was developed in the nineteenth century.

4oz (125g) butter	1½ teaspoons (1½ x 5ml)
4oz (125g) caster sugar	ground ginger
2 eggs	1–2 tablespoons (1–2 x 15ml)
4oz (125g) self-raising flour	cold water
Pinch of salt	3 tablespoons (3 x 15ml) golden
	syrup

Butter a 1½pt (750ml) pudding basin well. Cream butter and sugar together until pale and fluffy. Beat eggs and add a little at a time to creamed mixture, beating well between each addition. Sieve flour, salt and ginger together and carefully fold into mixture using a metal spoon. Add enough water to make a soft dropping consistency.

Spoon golden syrup into the buttered basin, then pour on the sponge mixture. Cover with buttered kitchen foil, making a pleat across the centre to allow pudding to rise. Tie foil firmly in place with string. Steam for 1½–2 hours or until firm and well risen, topping up with boiling water as necessary.

Remove from heat and leave to shrink slightly before turning out on to a warmed plate. Serve hot with Custard, Syrup, or Lemon Sauce, or with Honey and Brandy Iced Cream and clotted cream — particularly good for a summer dinner party.

Variations:
Marmalade Pudding
Replace golden syrup with marmalade of any flavour, and omit ginger if you wish. Serve with Marmalade Sauce.

Jam Pudding
Use jam instead of syrup and omit ginger. Serve with Jam Sauce.

My Mother's Ginger Pud *(serves 6)*
I remember this lovely suety pudding from my childhood. My mother adapted a recipe dated 1905 and came up with this 'rib-sticker'. It gives you a delicious warm feeling inside. Ginger dates back to Roman times when it was very popular. It is the root of the plant which has this unusual, hot sweet taste and is sold crystallised, preserved in syrup, green, whole, dried, or ground as in this recipe. It was much used in medieval recipes for both its flavour and preservative qualities, and also was the cheapest spice available along with cinnamon. It is used to flavour a large number of traditional puddings. If you are very fond of ginger, try adding a little chopped preserved ginger to this pudding before cooking.

4oz (125g) self-raising flour	4oz (125g) shredded suet
Pinch of salt	2 heaped tablespoons (2 x 15ml)
2 heaped teaspoons (2 x 5ml)	golden syrup
ground ginger	3 tablespoons (3 x 15ml) milk
4oz (125g) fresh white	1 level teaspoon (1 x 5ml)
breadcrumbs	bicarbonate of soda

Sieve flour, salt and ginger together into a mixing bowl. Stir in breadcrumbs and suet. Melt syrup over a gentle heat until just runny. Dissolve bicarbonate of soda in 3 tablespoons (3 x 15ml) milk and add to syrup. Pour into dry ingredients and mix well. Turn into a greased 1½pt (750ml) pudding basin. Cover with buttered kitchen foil making a pleat across the centre to allow room for pudding to rise. Tie securely with string and steam for 2–2½ hours until firm and well risen. Serve hot with Custard, Ginger or Syrup Sauce, or with whipped or clotted cream.

Traditional Plum Pudding *(makes 5 x 1lb [450g] puddings)*
Plum Pudding did not become associated with Christmas fare until the nineteenth century when Prince Albert introduced it, because he was so fond of this heavy rich pudding.

Plum porridge or pottage was the earliest form of plum pudding and dates back to medieval times. This was made from meat, usually shin of beef and veal, stewed together with currants, raisins, prunes (the dried plums which give their names to the mixture), spices, sugar, sack (a once popular wine from the Canary Islands), lemon juice and claret. The whole thing was thickened with brown breadcrumbs or sago. By the nineteenth century meat had been left out and the pudding became more like our modern-day Christmas pudding.

The idea of putting silver trinkets and charms into the pudding probably came from the earlier tradition of the beans inside the Twelfth Night Cake, but this has since died out. It is still traditional to bury a silver coin, if you have one, in the mixture. All the family should stir the pudding in turn on Stir Up Sunday, the Sunday before Advent, and make a wish at the same time. The coin should then be pushed in, plus a ring and a thimble; the coin is to bring worldly fortune, the ring a marriage and the thimble a life of blessedness.

8oz (225g) large prunes
½pt (250ml) cold tea
8oz (225g) currants
8oz (225g) sultanas
8oz (225g) large raisins
8oz (225g) self-raising flour
¼ teaspoon (¼ x 5ml) salt
½ teaspoon (½ x 5ml) baking powder
1 teaspoon (1 x 5ml) mixed spice
½ teaspoon (½ x 5ml) grated nutmeg
½ teaspoon (½ x 5ml) cinnamon
½ teaspoon (½ x 5ml) ground ginger
1lb (450g) fresh white breadcrumbs

8oz (225g) soft dark brown sugar
8oz (225g) shredded butcher's beef suet
2oz (50g) candied citron peel, chopped
2oz (50g) candied orange and lemon peel, finely chopped
4oz (125g) blanched almonds, chopped
Grated rind and juice of 1 orange
Grated rind and juice of 1 lemon
4oz (125g) carrots, grated
4oz (125g) cooking apple, grated
½pt (250ml) stout
3 eggs, beaten
Rum to mix, about 4 tablespoons (4 x 15ml)

Soak prunes overnight in cold tea. Next day, drain, remove stones and chop finely. The addition of prunes gives a richer, darker colour to the pudding as well as a very good flavour. Wash and dry all remaining dried fruit and stone raisins if necessary.

Sieve flour, salt, baking powder and spices together into a very large bowl. Add breadcrumbs, sugar and suet, mixing in each ingredient thoroughly. Gradually mix in all the dried fruit, candied peel and nuts. Stir in the rind and juice of the lemon and orange, followed by grated carrot and apple. Pour in the stout and mix until smooth. Cover basin with a clean cloth and leave in a cool place overnight or longer if convenient (the flavour will be improved). In fact, the mixture can be left to stand for a fortnight or longer at this point. Stir mixture every day if you decide to do this.

On the day you want to cook the puddings, add the beaten eggs. Stir furiously until the pudding ingredients are thoroughly blended. Add enough rum to make a soft dropping consistency. Spoon mixture into greased pudding basins to come within 1in (2½cm) of rim, packing mixture down well with the back of a wooden spoon. You will need 5 x 1lb (450g) basins or 2 x 2lb (900g) and 1 x 1lb (450g) basins. Cover the top of each with greased greaseproof paper. Put a thick layer of flour on top of the greaseproof paper, pressing it down well. (This will become a solid paste and act as a seal both for cooking and storing.) Then cover with another piece of greaseproof paper. Finally, cover basins with a pudding cloth, muslin or aluminium foil, making a pleat in the centre to allow room for puddings to rise during cooking. Tie securely with string and make a handle of string across the top of each basin, so that you can lift the puddings in and out of the pan easily.

Place puddings in a steamer, double boiler, or in a large pan of gently boiling water. Steam for at least 6 hours, topping up water level from time to time with boiling water. When cooked, remove puddings from pan and leave until cold. Renew top piece of greaseproof paper and cloth and store in a cool dry place until needed.

On the great day, steam again for 2–3 hours before serving. Turn out on to a large platter. Sprinkle with icing sugar. Heat some brandy, whisky, rum or Kirsch in a small saucepan or ladle. Pour over pudding and set alight. Bring the pudding to the table, burning, and surrounded by a hedge of holly. Any spirit can be used, but you will find that rum burns longer. Make sure your holly doesn't go up in smoke!

Granny's Leg *(serves 6)*

Also called Spotted Dog, is a suet roly-poly pudding studded with currants — everybody's idea of a nursery treat and I know there are many men who yearn to sink their teeth into this pudding once again! Originally this pudding was boiled in a floured cloth and you can still cook it in this way. It appeared as the first course of a meal to take the edge off the appetite until the end of the nineteenth century, in the same way as Yorkshire Pudding, and any left over was served with the vegetables and meat to make them go further.

6oz (175g) self-raising flour
Pinch of salt
3oz (75g) shredded suet
2oz (50g) caster sugar

6oz (175g) currants
4–6 tablespoons (4–6 x 15ml)
  milk

Sieve flour and salt together into a mixing bowl. Stir in suet, sugar and currants. Mix in sufficient milk to make a soft dough. Roll out on a floured board to an oblong shape and roll up like a Swiss roll. Wrap loosely in buttered and pleated greaseproof paper and then in pleated kitchen foil so that the pudding has room to expand to keep it light. Steam in a large saucepan or fish-kettle of boiling water for 2 hours.

When cooked, unwrap pudding, turn out on to a hot dish and serve very hot with Custard Sauce or brown sugar and melted butter.

Guard's Pudding *(serves 6)*

Originally known as Burbridge Pudding and said to be a favourite of the Guards, hence its new name. It is a very traditional English steamed pudding, made with raspberry jam, and will certainly please the menfolk.

6oz (175g) fresh brown or white
  breadcrumbs
6oz (175g) shredded suet
4oz (125g) soft brown sugar
1 large egg or 2 small eggs

4 tablespoons (4 x 15ml)
  raspberry jam
Grated rind and juice of 1 lemon
1 level teaspoon (1 x 5ml)
  bicarbonate of soda

Mix breadcrumbs, suet and sugar together in a bowl. Beat egg or eggs with jam and lemon rind. Dissolve bicarbonate of soda in lemon juice and add to egg mixture. Stir into dry ingredients thoroughly. Spoon mixture into a well-buttered 2pt (1 litre) pudding basin. Cover with well-buttered foil making a pleat across the centre to allow pudding to rise. Tie down securely with string and steam for 2½ hours or until well risen and firm.

Allow to shrink slightly before turning out on to a warmed serving plate. Serve pudding hot with pouring or clotted cream, or Custard, Jam or fresh Raspberry Sauce.

Hunters Pudding *(serves 6)*

Also called Hunt Pudding, this comes from Sussex. It is another name for Plum Duff which is a pudding popular all over the country dating back to the early nineteenth century. Duff was a colloquial expression for dough. This pudding is a mixture of raisins, currants, suet and redcurrant jelly.

3oz (75g) self-raising flour
Pinch of salt
½ teaspoon (½ x 5ml) mixed
   spice
2oz (50g) fresh white or brown
   breadcrumbs
3oz (75g) shredded suet

2oz (50g) caster or brown sugar
3oz (75g) raisins
3oz (75g) currants
4oz (125g) redcurrant jelly
¼pt (150ml) milk
1 tablespoon (1 x 15ml) brandy
   (optional)

Well butter a 2pt (1 litre) pudding basin. Sieve flour, salt and mixed spice together into mixing bowl. Add breadcrumbs, suet, sugar and fruit and stir. Stir in redcurrant jelly and mix with milk and brandy, if using, to a fairly soft dough.

Put mixture into prepared pudding basin and cover with buttered kitchen foil, making a pleat across the centre to allow pudding to rise. Tie down firmly with string. Steam for 2–2½ hours until well risen and firm, filling the saucepan with more boiling water as necessary.

When cooked, remove from pan and turn out on to a warm serving plate. Serve with Custard, Madeira or Lemon Sauce.

A Kentish Well Pudding *(serves 6)*

Kent and Sussex extend their rivalry to puddings — the most famous being Kentish Well Pudding and Sussex Pond Pudding. The former consists of a suet crust enclosing butter, brown sugar, currants and a whole lemon, and in the latter the currants are omitted. Either way, when the pudding is cut open, a rich, sweet syrup oozes out — the well or pond.

8oz (225g) self-raising flour
Pinch of salt
1oz (25g) caster sugar
4oz (125g) shredded suet
Grated rind of 1 large lemon
6–8 tablespoons (6–8 x 15ml)
   cold water

2–3 cloves
1 large thin-skinned lemon
4oz (125g) unsalted softened
   butter
4oz (125g) soft dark brown sugar
4–6oz (125–175g) currants

Sieve flour and salt together into a mixing bowl. Stir in sugar. Add suet and 1 teaspoon (1 x 5ml) grated lemon rind. Add just sufficient water to mix to a soft, but not sticky, dough using a palette knife. Roll out on a lightly floured board. Well butter a 2pt (1 litre) pudding basin and line with suet crust, reserving about one-third of pastry for the lid. Sprinkle the remaining lemon rind into the bottom of the basin. Press cloves into thin-skinned lemon (it is essential that your lemon should be juicy and thin skinned to get the full flavour). Prick lemon all over with a darning or trussing needle. Pat softened butter around lemon and roll in dark brown sugar. Place coated lemon in lined basin and pack currants around it, plus any remaining butter and sugar. The basin should be full. (If your lemon is a bit large you may have to cut the end off.) Dampen pastry edges and fit the lid. Seal well by pressing edges together. Cover with buttered kitchen foil, making a pleat across the centre to allow pudding to rise. Tie down securely with string. Steam for 3–3½ hours or until suet is cooked and well risen. Allow to rest for a few minutes before turning out on to a warmed serving plate. When cut, the delicious buttery 'pond' flows out. Serve either with a segment of lemon from the centre of the pudding, and with Custard or Lemon Sauce, or with whipped or clotted cream.

A Steamed Lemon Pudding *(serves 6)*

A few citrus fruits began to arrive in Britain in the thirteenth century from the Mediterranean — lemons, oranges, which were of the bitter Seville type, and a few pomegranates. By the end of the Tudor period, lemons were being imported in large quantities and used in perfumes as well as for flavouring food. They have continued in popularity over the centuries. This pudding is very light and a refreshing end to a rich meal.

1 slice lemon or orange	5oz (150g) self-raising flour
1 rounded tablespoon (1 x 15ml) home-made or good quality bought lemon or orange curd	Pinch of salt
	1 level teaspoon (1 x 5ml) baking powder
4oz (125g) unsalted butter	3 tablespoons (3 x 15ml) lemon or orange juice
4oz (125g) caster sugar	
2 large eggs	
Grated rind of 2 lemons or oranges	

Well butter a 2pt (1 litre) pudding basin. Place slice of lemon or orange in the bottom of the basin and cover it with lemon or orange curd. Cream butter and sugar together until pale and fluffy. Beat eggs and beat into mixture a teaspoonful at a time. Add lemon or orange rind. Sieve flour, salt and baking powder together and gradually fold into creamed mixture. Mix to a soft dropping consistency with the lemon or orange juice. Spoon mixture into prepared basin. Cover with a piece of buttered foil making a pleat across the top of the basin. Tie firmly with string and steam in a large saucepan with boiling water coming halfway up the basin or in a prepared steamer. Steam, with water boiling at a steady roll, topping up with more *boiling* water as necessary, for about 1½ hours.

Turn out pudding on to a hot plate — don't leave the lovely lemony topping behind in the basin! Serve hot with Custard, Lemon or Orange Sauce.

Orange and Treacle Sponge Pudding *(serves 6)*

3 tablespoons (3 x 15ml) golden syrup	4oz (125g) caster sugar
	2 eggs
Grated rind and juice of 2 oranges	4oz (125g) self-raising flour
2 tablespoons (2 x 15ml) fresh white breadcrumbs	About 1 tablespoon (1 x 15ml) cold water
4oz (125g) unsalted butter	

Well butter a 1½pt (750ml) pudding basin. Put golden syrup, rind of 1 orange, and juice of 2 oranges into a small heavy saucepan. Warm gently to make a runny sauce. Fold in breadcrumbs and pour sauce into the bottom of prepared basin.

Cream butter and sugar together until pale and fluffy. Beat eggs and add a little at a time to creamed mixture. Sieve flour and gently fold into mixture using a metal spoon. Stir in rind of second orange and enough water to make a soft dropping consistency. Pour mixture into the basin and cover with buttered kitchen foil making a pleat across the top of the basin. Tie down firmly with string. Steam for about 1½ hours until well risen and firm.

Turn out on to a warmed serving plate and serve with Orange or Custard Sauce, or Honey and Brandy Iced Cream, and clotted cream.

Pear and Walnut Pudding *(serves 6)*

This is really a Pear and Walnut Hat Pudding — a suet crust filled with juicy pears and chopped walnuts, which have been used together in pies and puddings, both savoury and sweet, for centuries. In this recipe they are flavoured with coriander, which has been used in British cooking since Elizabethan times when it was rubbed into cooked meat to act as a preservative. It has a mild spicy orangy flavour. Other fruit fillings are just as successful — try gooseberries, plums, apricots, greengages, rhubarb, damsons, cherries, blackcurrants, or dried apricots and prunes.

8oz (225g) self-raising flour	2oz (50g) chopped walnuts
Pinch of salt	Grated rind and juice of 1 orange
4oz (125g) shredded suet	3oz (75g) brown sugar
6–8 tablespoons (6–8 x 15ml) cold water	6 crushed coriander seeds
	2oz (50g) unsalted butter
1½lb (675g) cooking pears	

Well butter a 2pt (1 litre) pudding basin. Sieve flour and salt together into a mixing bowl. Stir in suet and mix with sufficient cold water to make a soft light dough. Knead lightly and roll out on a floured board about ¼in (6mm) thick. Use two-thirds of the pastry to line prepared basin.

Peel, core and slice pears and fill the lined basin with layers of pears, chopped walnuts, grated orange rind and juice, brown sugar and coriander. Add butter, cut into small pieces. Cover the basin with the reserved piece of pastry, dampening edges and pressing together firmly. Cover with a piece of buttered greaseproof paper pleated across the centre, followed by a piece of buttered kitchen foil, again pleated across the centre. Tie down firmly with string. Steam for 2–2½ hours, topping up with boiling water as necessary.

Turn out on to a warmed serving plate. Serve hot with clotted cream and brown sugar or with Custard Sauce.

Shirt-sleeve Pudding *(serves 6)*

This is a rolled suet jam pudding which was boiled in a cloth. In Victorian days it was customary to keep an old shirt-sleeve for the purpose — hence the name of this pudding. It is also called Jam Roly-poly or Suety Jack. Mincemeat, golden syrup or black treacle can be used instead of jam.

6oz (175g) self-raising flour	Juice of 1 lemon made up to
Pinch of salt	4 tablespoons (4 x 15ml) with
3oz (75g) shredded suet	cold water
Grated rind of ½ lemon	6–8oz (175–225g) blackcurrant
1 egg	jam

Half-fill a steamer, large saucepan or fish-kettle with water and put on to boil. Grease a piece of kitchen foil 8in x 12in (20cm x 30cm).

Sieve flour and salt together into a mixing bowl and stir in suet and lemon rind. Beat egg and add to lemon juice and water. Stir this liquid into flour mixture using a palette knife until a soft dough is formed. Roll out on a floured board to a rectangle 8in x 12in (20cm x 30cm). Spread thickly with jam leaving a 1in (2½cm) border all the way round the edges. Brush edges with milk and roll up evenly, starting from one short side. Pinch the ends well to seal and keep in the jam. Place roll on prepared foil and wrap round loosely, making several pleats in the foil to allow room for expansion. This helps keep the pudding light. Seal edges of foil well, so that water cannot get in.

Place pudding roll in prepared steamer. Cover and steam in steadily boiling water for 1½–2 hours, topping up with more boiling water as necessary. When cooked, remove from foil and serve very hot with Custard Sauce. Do be careful of the jam when you eat the pudding — it will be very hot!

Snowdon Pudding *(serves 6)*

This pudding was adopted by Prince Albert when he came over to England and called Albert Pudding; but this caused a controversy, endangering the peace between England and Wales! It was said very unkindly that 'a *bad* Albert Pudding will make a *good* Snowdon Pudding'. However, the original pudding named after the Welsh mountain is much older and brought much fame to the hotel at the foot of Snowdon where it was served to hungry climbers and walkers. Basically, it is a sponge pudding with sultanas or raisins and lemon rind, originally steamed in a fancy mould lined with orange and lemon shapes and angelica, and served with a wine sauce.

4oz (125g) raisins or sultanas	Pinch of salt
1oz (25g) chopped angelica	1oz (25g) brown sugar
4oz (125g) fresh white	Grated rind of 1 lemon
breadcrumbs	3oz (75g) lemon marmalade
1oz (25g) ground rice or rice	2 eggs
flour	3–4 tablespoons (3–4 x 15ml)
4oz (125g) shredded suet	milk

Well butter a 2pt (1 litre) pudding basin. Sprinkle 1 tablespoon (1 x 15ml) raisins or sultanas and chopped angelica over the bottom of buttered basin. Mix together the rest of the raisins or sultanas with dry ingredients and lemon rind. Stir in marmalade. Beat eggs and add to mixture with enough milk to make a soft dropping consistency. Spoon carefully into prepared basin. Cover with buttered foil with a generous pleat across the top. Tie down with string and steam for 2 hours until well risen, topping up with *boiling* water from time to time.

Allow to shrink slightly before unmoulding on to a warmed serving plate. Serve very hot with Madeira or Lemon Sauce.

Spotted Dick *(serves 6)*

In this version, butter is used instead of the traditional suet, which gives a lighter pudding. Currants only should be used to be traditional. Also known as Alma Pudding.

8oz (225g) self-raising flour	6oz (175g) currants
Pinch of salt	2 eggs
4oz (125g) butter or margarine	About 1 tablespoon (1 x 15ml)
2 heaped tablespoons	milk or cold water
(2 x 15ml) caster sugar	

Butter well a 1½pt (750ml) pudding basin. Sieve flour and salt into a bowl. Rub in butter or margarine and stir in sugar and currants. Beat eggs and add to mixture. Stir until smooth and add enough milk to give a soft dropping consistency. Pour into buttered basin, cover with buttered kitchen foil making a pleat across the centre to allow pudding to rise. Tie securely with string and steam for 1½–2 hours or until well risen and firm.

Turn out on to a warmed serving plate. Serve very hot with Syrup, Lemon or Custard Sauce.

Variation:
Ginger Spotted Dick
Sieve ½ teaspoon (½ x 5ml) ground ginger with flour and salt and add 2 pieces of finely chopped preserved ginger to the currants.

Tiverton Batter Pudding *(serves 6–8)* *

Steamed batter puddings have been very popular for generations but seem to have lost favour in more recent years, probably because most of us like the baked version so much. This lemony batter pudding comes from the West Country. For a different flavour use the grated rind of an orange instead of the lemon.

8oz (225g) plain flour	4 eggs, separated
½ level teaspoon (½ x 5ml) salt	1pt (500ml) milk
Grated rind of 1 lemon	1oz (25g) butter

Well butter a 3pt (1½ litre) pudding basin. Sieve flour and salt together and add lemon rind. Make a well in the centre of the dry ingredients. Add egg yolks and beat gradually into flour mixture. Add milk a little at a time, beating continuously until a smooth batter is formed. Melt the butter in a small saucepan and stir into batter. Cover and leave in a cool place for at least 30 minutes.

Whisk egg whites until stiff and standing in peaks. Fold gently into batter and pour into the prepared pudding basin. Cover with buttered kitchen foil, making a pleat across the centre to allow room for pudding to rise. Tie down securely with string and steam for 2 hours, topping up with boiling water as necessary, until well risen and firm to the touch.

Turn out on to a warmed serving dish. Serve immediately with Lemon, Custard, Madeira or Jam Sauce.

Variation:
Strawberry Batter Pudding *
Put 8oz (225g) small strawberries into the bottom of the prepared basin before adding pudding mixture, and use grated orange rind instead of lemon.

A Treacle Duff *(serves 6)*

Black treacle was traditionally layered with suet pastry in this pudding, but golden syrup is more to our taste now. Do try the traditional way if you are a lover of black treacle, or use jam or marmalade. Duff is a colloquial term for dough.

8oz (225g) self-raising flour
¼ teaspoon (¼ x 5ml) salt
4oz (125g) shredded suet
Grated rind of ½ lemon

Juice of 1 lemon made up to
6 tablespoons (6 x 15ml) with
water
5 tablespoons (5 x 15ml) golden
syrup

Well butter a 2–2½pt (1–1¼ litre) pudding basin. Sieve flour and salt together into a mixing bowl and stir in the suet and lemon rind. Stir lemon juice and water into the flour mixture using a palette knife to make a soft dough. Turn on to a floured board and divide into 4 portions, each a little larger than the next. Pat the smallest portion of dough into a circle large enough to fit the bottom of the prepared pudding basin. Spoon 1 tablespoon (1 x 15ml) golden syrup over it. Pat next portion of dough into a circle to fit the basin and spoon over 2 tablespoons (2 x 15ml) golden syrup. Continue like this ending with a top layer of suet pastry. Cover with buttered kitchen foil with a good pleat across the centre to allow pudding to rise. Tie down firmly with string, and steam for 2½ hours, topping up with boiling water as necessary.

Turn out on to a warmed serving plate and serve very hot with Custard or Lemon Sauce, or with pouring cream.

A Walnut and Date Pudding *(serves 6)*
Very popular from the early nineteenth century.

4oz (125g) roughly chopped
dates
1 tablespoon (1 x 15ml) rum
3oz (75g) self-raising flour
Pinch of salt
½ teaspoon (½ x 5ml) mixed
spice
3oz (75g) fresh white or brown
breadcrumbs

3oz (75g) shredded suet
2 heaped tablespoons (2 x 15ml)
soft brown sugar
2oz (50g) roughly chopped
walnuts
2 eggs
1–2 tablespoons (1–2 x 15ml)
milk or water

Soak chopped dates in the rum while you prepare pudding. Well butter a 1½pt (750ml) pudding basin.

Sieve flour, salt and spice together into a bowl. Stir in breadcrumbs, suet, sugar, chopped walnuts and dates, including rum. Beat eggs and add to pudding mixture with enough milk to make a soft dropping consistency.

Turn pudding mixture into a buttered basin and cover with buttered kitchen foil, making a pleat across the centre to allow pudding to rise. Tie securely with string. Steam for 2 hours.

Serve very hot with a Hard Sauce or Custard Sauce, or clotted cream.

SWEET SAUCES AND BISCUITS TO ACCOMPANY PUDDINGS

Apricot Sauce

4 tablespoons (4 x 15ml) apricot
  jam
1 tablespoon (1 x 15ml) water

1 teaspoon (1 x 5ml) lemon juice
1 tablespoon (1 x 15ml) brandy
  (optional)

Melt jam in a saucepan with water and lemon juice. Add brandy if using. Rub through a sieve.

Butterscotch Sauce

1oz (25g) butter
2 level tablespoons (2 x 15ml)
  golden syrup

6oz (175g) soft brown sugar
4 tablespoons (4 x 15ml) single
  cream

Melt butter, golden syrup and sugar together in a small saucepan. Bring to the boil. Stir in cream and heat again.

Chocolate Sauce

$\frac{1}{2}$oz (12g) cornflour
$\frac{1}{4}$pt (150ml) water
3oz (75g) Menier (or good
  quality) plain chocolate

1oz (25g) caster sugar
2–3 drops vanilla essence

Mix cornflour to a smooth paste with a little of the water. Put the rest of the water and chocolate, broken into pieces, in a small saucepan over gentle heat and melt. Bring slowly to the boil and then remove from heat. Stir in cornflour mixture and bring back to the boil. Add sugar and vanilla essence to taste.

Coffee Sauce

4oz (125g) demerara sugar
2 tablespoons (2 x 15ml) water

$\frac{1}{2}$pt (250ml) strong black coffee
2 tablespoons (2 x 15ml)
  Tia Maria

Dissolve the sugar in the water by heating gently in a saucepan. When the sugar has dissolved, boil rapidly until syrup becomes golden in colour. Add coffee and Tia Maria. Boil for a few minutes until syrupy.

Custard Sauce

½pt (250ml) milk
¼pt (150ml) single cream
1 vanilla pod or strip of lemon
   peel
3 eggs

2 level tablespoons (2 x 15ml)
   caster sugar
2 heaped teaspoons (2 x 5ml)
   cornflour
4 tablespoons (4 x 15ml) milk

Heat milk and cream in a saucepan (you can use all milk if you prefer) with vanilla pod or lemon peel. Bring to the boil. Remove from heat and leave to cool for a few seconds, removing vanilla pod or lemon peel. Beat eggs with sugar in a basin. Mix cornflour with 4 tablespoons (4 x 15ml) milk until a smooth paste. Add this to the egg mixture and stir well. Pour hot milk slowly on to egg mixture, stirring continuously. Rinse out the saucepan, leaving a film of cold water in the bottom. Return custard to pan and stir with a wooden spoon over a low heat until thick. (Don't boil your custard or it will curdle.)

Strain into a jug or bowl and serve hot. (If you don't want a skin to form on top of your custard, sprinkle the surface with caster sugar or cover closely with a piece of wetted greaseproof paper or cling film.)

Variations:
Brandy Custard Sauce
Add 1 tablespoon (1 x 15ml) brandy to your custard sauce.

Almond Custard Sauce
Add a few drops of almond essence instead of vanilla pod.

Lemon Custard Sauce
Add grated rind of 1 lemon.

Economical Custard Sauce

This more economical version of custard sauce is still much nicer than the bright yellow custard powder you can buy, and there is less chance of it curdling because the cornflour makes it more stable.

1pt (500ml) milk
Vanilla pod or vanilla essence
2 egg yolks

2oz (50g) granulated sugar
1 tablespoon (1 x 15ml)
   cornflour

Put milk and vanilla pod, if using, into a heavy saucepan and bring slowly to the boil. Leave to cool a little and allow the vanilla pod to infuse. Beat egg yolks and sugar together until pale, and blend in cornflour. Gradually stir in the hot milk, beating continuously. Add 2 or 3 drops vanilla essence, if not using a vanilla pod. Rinse out the milk pan, leaving a film of cold water in the bottom. Return custard to the pan and stir over very gentle heat until thickened. Do not bring to the boil. Serve immediately in a warmed jug.

Ginger Sauce

2 pieces preserved stem ginger
1 tablespoon (1 x 15ml) caster
  sugar

1 tablespoon (1 x 15ml) dark rum
¼pt (150ml) double cream

Chop ginger very finely. Mix with sugar and rum. Stir in double cream and continue stirring until thick. Chill before serving.

Jam Sauce

3 tablespoons (3 x 15ml)
  raspberry, strawberry, plum,
  apricot or blackcurrant jam

6 tablespoons (6 x 15ml) water
1 teaspoon (1 x 5ml) lemon juice

Melt the jam in a saucepan with water and lemon juice. Push through a sieve to make a smooth sauce. Serve hot.

Lemon or Orange Sauce

4 tablespoons (4 x 15ml) home-
  made lemon or orange curd

¼pt (150ml) single cream

Mix lemon or orange curd and cream together. Heat in a saucepan over a low heat until hot but not boiling. Serve in a warmed jug.

Eliza Acton's Madeira Sauce

Finely pared rind of ½ lemon
¼pt (150ml) water
2oz (50g) soft brown sugar
1oz (25g) butter

2 level teaspoons (2 x 5ml)
  cornflour
¼pt (150ml) Madeira or sweet
  sherry

Simmer lemon rind, water and sugar in a saucepan for 10–15 minutes. Strain to remove lemon rind. Return syrup to saucepan. Work butter and cornflour together in a small basin. Add small pieces of this creamed mixture to hot syrup to thicken. Add Madeira or sherry, and reheat, but don't boil. Serve hot in a warmed sauceboat.

Marmalade Sauce

Juice of 1 orange
1 level teaspoon (1 x 5ml)
  cornflour
½pt (250ml) white wine

4 heaped tablespoons (4 x 15ml)
  marmalade
2 tablespoons (2 x 15ml) soft
  brown sugar

Dissolve cornflour in orange juice. Heat wine, marmalade and sugar in a saucepan until the sugar has dissolved, stirring from time to time. Stir in cornflour mixture and bring to boil, stirring well. Simmer for 2 minutes. Serve hot.

Orange and Lemon Sauce

½oz (12g) cornflour
½pt (250ml) milk
Grated rind and juice of 1 lemon

Grated rind and juice of 1 orange
3 tablespoons (3 x 15ml) golden syrup

Mix cornflour to a paste with 3 tablespoons (3 x 15ml) of the milk. Pour remaining milk into a saucepan and heat gently. Add the lemon and orange rind. Pour hot milk slowly on to cornflour, stirring continuously. Return sauce to pan and simmer for 3 minutes, stirring gently. Stir in fruit juices and golden syrup.

Port Wine Sauce

Grated rind of 1 orange
¼pt (150ml) water
2oz (50g) soft brown sugar
1oz (25g) unsalted butter
2 level teaspoons (2 x 5ml) cornflour

¼pt (150ml) ruby or tawny port
½ teaspoon (½ x 5ml) grated nutmeg
1 tablespoon (1 x 15ml) orange juice

Put orange rind, water and sugar in a saucepan and bring to the boil. Simmer for 15 minutes. Cream butter and cornflour together until smooth and add to syrup in small pieces. Stir briskly and then add port, nutmeg and orange juice. Heat until almost boiling and serve.

Raspberry Sauce

8oz (225g) fresh raspberries
3oz (75g) caster sugar

Juice of 1 lemon
2 tablespoons (2 x 15ml) water

Heat all ingredients in a saucepan over a very low heat. Simmer gently for 5 minutes. Rub through a sieve. Taste for sweetness.

Red Cherry Sauce

1lb (450g) red cherries
2oz (50g) sugar
¼ teaspoon (¼ x 5ml) ground cinnamon

¼pt (150ml) water
1 dessertspoon (1 x 10ml) arrowroot
1 tablespoon (1 x 15ml) water

Stone cherries and put into a saucepan with sugar and cinnamon. Cover with lid and set on a low heat until the juice runs freely, then remove cherries with a draining spoon. Add water to juice, and boil gently for 4–5 minutes. Taste for sweetness and add more sugar if necessary. Dissolve arrowroot in 1 tablespoon (1 x 15ml) water and add to cherry juice. Bring back to boil — the sauce should be smooth and the consistency of cream. Put cherries back in the saucepan and reheat if you want to serve the sauce hot.

Rum Sauce

8oz (225g) caster sugar
3oz (75g) unsalted butter

2 eggs, separated
1 tablespoon (1 x 15ml) dark rum

Cream sugar and butter together. Put into the top of a double sauce-pan or into a basin fitting snugly over a saucepan of simmering water. Beat egg yolks and add to creamed mixture. Place over a gentle heat and stir until thick enough to coat the back of a wooden spoon. Beat egg whites until stiff and fold carefully into sauce. Add rum. Serve hot.

Syrup Sauce

4 tablespoons (4 x 15ml) golden
  syrup

2 tablespoons (2 x 15ml) water
Juice of ½ lemon

Simmer syrup and water together in a small saucepan for 2 or 3 minutes. Add lemon juice and serve hot.

Treacle Cream Sauce

4 tablespoons (4 x 15ml) treacle
  or golden syrup

¼pt (150ml) single cream

Melt treacle or syrup in a small saucepan. Add cream and heat until almost boiling. Serve hot.

HARD SAUCES

Brandy and Lemon Butter

4oz (125g) unsalted butter
4oz (125g) caster sugar
½ teaspoon (½ x 5ml) grated
  lemon rind
1 tablespoon (1 x 15ml) boiling
  water

1 teaspoon (1 x 5ml) lemon juice
4 tablespoons (4 x 15ml) brandy
Extra grated lemon rind for
  decoration

Cut the butter into small pieces and put with sugar and lemon rind in a warmed bowl. Beat until creamy. Add boiling water and continue to beat until every grain of sugar has dissolved. (This will prevent sauce from tasting gritty.) Add lemon juice and brandy a little at a time, beating continuously to stop sauce curdling. When completely blended, put in a pretty dish and store in refrigerator until needed.

Variations:
Add a few chopped glacé cherries and angelica to sauce.

Add a little chopped crystallised or preserved stem ginger to sauce.

Georgian Fairy Butter

The Georgians served this on its own as a sweet, but we would find it too rich. It is, however, delicious served with Christmas pudding or mince pies instead of brandy butter. Use it at other times of the year as a cake filling or to decorate cold puddings. It is very good as a filling for meringues and small choux buns.

4oz (125g) ratafia biscuits
3 tablespoons (3 x 15ml) sweet sherry or brandy
4oz (125g) unsalted butter
2oz (50g) caster sugar
3 hard-boiled egg yolks

1 tablespoon (1 x 15ml) orange flower water, brandy, rum or lemon juice
1 teaspoon (1 x 5ml) very finely grated orange rind
½oz (12g) flaked almonds for decoration

Line a pretty serving dish with ratafias, reserving a few for decoration, soaked in sherry or brandy.

Cream butter and sugar together. Mash egg yolks and beat into creamed mixture with chosen flavouring. Pass through a sieve and carefully pile into dish with ratafias, using 2 forks. This way you will not destroy the 'fairy' texture. Scatter finely grated orange rind over your Fairy Butter and serve decorated with ratafias and flaked almonds.

This butter can be made 2 or 3 days before you need it and kept in a cool place.

Rum and Orange Butter

4oz (125g) unsalted butter
4oz (125g) soft brown sugar
½ teaspoon (½ x 5ml) grated orange rind
1 tablespoon (1 x 15ml) boiling water

1 teaspoon (1 x 5ml) orange juice
4 tablespoons (4 x 15ml) dark rum
Extra grated orange rind for decoration

Make exactly as Brandy and Lemon Butter, substituting orange rind and juice for lemon, and rum for brandy. Serve chilled, sprinkled with grated orange rind.

Variations:
Add a few chopped glacé cherries and angelica to sauce.

Add a little chopped crystallised or preserved stem ginger to sauce.

Senior Wrangler Sauce

4oz (125g) unsalted butter
4oz (125g) caster sugar
2oz (50g) ground almonds
1 tablespoon (1 x 15ml) boiling
  water

4 tablespoons (4 x 15ml) brandy
A few drops of almond essence

Cut the butter into small pieces and put with sugar in a warmed bowl. Beat until creamy. Add ground almonds and boiling water and continue to beat until every grain of sugar has dissolved. (This will prevent sauce from tasting gritty.) Gradually add brandy and almond essence, beating continuously. Serve very cold with rich fruit, steamed and plain sponge puddings.

Almond Tiles *(makes about 18)*
These are known as 'tiles' because they are curved like some roof tiles. Walnuts or hazelnuts can be used instead of almonds for a change.

3oz (75g) unsalted butter
3oz (75g) caster sugar
2oz (50g) plain flour

Pinch of salt
3oz (75g) finely shredded
  blanched almonds

Soften butter, add sugar and cream together well, until light and fluffy. Sieve flour with salt and stir into the creamed mixture. Add finely shredded almonds and mix well. Put mixture, a teaspoon (1 x 5ml) at a time, on to a well-buttered baking tray and flatten with a wet fork. Leave plenty of room between biscuits as they will spread during cooking. Bake in a moderately hot oven (400°F, 200°C; Gas Mark 6) for 6–8 minutes or until just coloured. Remove from oven and leave to harden for a few seconds, before removing with a palette knife. Curl quickly round a rolling pin and leave to set. Remove and leave to cool on a wire rack. Store in an airtight tin until needed.

Brandy Snaps *(makes about 20)*
These biscuits are traditionally flavoured with brandy, but lemon juice can be used instead. They are delicious filled with whipped cream and served with fools, fruit, junkets, jellies, iced creams and milk puddings.

4 level tablespoons (4 x 15ml)
  golden syrup
4oz (125g) butter
4oz (125g) caster sugar
4oz (125g) plain flour

1½ teaspoons (1½ x 5ml)
  ground ginger
2 teaspoons (2 x 5ml) brandy or
  lemon juice
Grated rind of 1 lemon

Lightly butter 3 baking trays and some wooden spoon handles.
Put syrup, butter and caster sugar into a heavy saucepan and stir over gentle heat until the sugar has dissolved. Remove from heat and beat in sieved flour and ginger. Stir in brandy or lemon juice and grated lemon rind. Drop 3 or 4 spoonfuls of mixture 4in (10cm) apart on a baking tray. (The biscuits will spread during cooking.) Bake in the centre of a moderate oven (350°F, 180°C; Gas Mark 4) for 7–10 minutes or until golden in colour. When cooked, allow biscuits to cool on the baking tray for 2 minutes to harden a little, then loosen with a palette knife and wind around a wooden spoon handle. Leave to set, and then gently slide off handles and cool on wire tray. Bake remaining mixture in the same way, using a cold baking tray for each batch. (If biscuits are difficult to shape, put them back in the oven to soften.)

Cats' Tongues *(makes about 20)*

2oz (50g) unsalted butter	2 egg whites
2oz (50g) caster sugar	2oz (50g) plain flour
A few drops vanilla essence	

Lightly grease and flour a baking tray.
Cream butter with a wooden spoon until soft. Beat in caster sugar and vanilla essence until light and fluffy. Gradually beat in unbeaten egg whites, a teaspoon (1 x 5ml) at a time. Sieve flour and fold gently into the mixture. Using a piping bag with a plain ½in (1cm) nozzle, pipe the mixture on to the prepared baking tray in 3in (7½cm) lengths. Leave at least 1in (2½cm) space between each biscuit to allow room for them to spread during cooking. Bake near the top of a hot oven (425°F, 220°C; Gas Mark 7) for 6–8 minutes or until golden and tinged with brown around the edges. Remove from the oven and leave on the baking tray for a couple of minutes to harden, then remove and cool on a wire rack. When cold, store in an airtight tin to keep them crisp.

Cigarette Biscuits *(makes about 15)*

2 egg whites	2oz (50g) plain flour
2½oz (60g) caster sugar	2–3 drops vanilla essence
2oz (50g) unsalted butter	

Lightly grease 3 baking trays. Beat egg whites until frothy, add caster sugar and beat again for a few minutes until thick and smooth. Melt butter and gently fold into mixture with the sieved flour. Flavour with vanilla essence. Put 3 teaspoons (3 x 5ml) of the mixture on to a baking tray and spread each into an oval shape. Bake near the top of a fairly hot oven (400°F, 200°C; Gas Mark 6) for 5–6 minutes, or until lightly brown round the edges. Remove from the oven and leave to stand for 2 seconds to harden a little, then remove biscuits from the tray with a palette knife, and curl each one tightly round the handle of a wooden spoon or pencil. Allow to set in shape for 2–3 minutes before removing and cooling on a wire rack until completely cold. Cook remaining biscuit mixture in the same way, using a cool baking tray for each batch. Store when cold in an airtight tin.

Macaroons *(makes about 36)*

If you want to make ratafias instead of macaroons, use the same mixture, but pipe very small rounds on to the rice paper.

6oz (175g) ground almonds	A few drops of almond or vanilla
1oz (25g) icing sugar	essence
1 teaspoon (1 x 5ml) ground rice	Caster sugar for sprinkling
8oz (225g) granulated sugar	1oz (25g) blanched almonds
3 egg whites	

Line 2 large baking sheets with rice paper or Bakewell paper. Mix ground almonds, sieved icing sugar, ground rice and granulated sugar together in a mixing bowl. Stir in unbeaten egg whites and almond or vanilla essence. Continue stirring until thoroughly mixed. Pipe out 2in (5cm) rounds of the mixture on to the prepared baking sheets, using a piping bag fitted with a ¾in (2cm) plain nozzle or use a teaspoon to pile on rounds of the mixture. Allow plenty of room between each biscuit for them to spread during cooking. Sprinkle each biscuit with caster sugar and top with half a blanched almond.

Bake biscuits for about 25 minutes in a cool oven (300°F, 150°C; Gas Mark 2), or until very light brown. Leave to cool, then store in an airtight tin.

Orange and Almond Crisps *(makes about 18)*

These are a delicious accompaniment to fruit salads and fools and many other cold puddings. Try using candied lemon or citron peel for a change.

3oz (75g) unsalted butter	3oz (75g) chopped blanched
3oz (75g) caster sugar	almonds
2oz (50g) plain flour	3oz (75g) chopped candied
Pinch of salt	orange peel
	2 teaspoons (2 x 5ml) milk

Soften butter, add sugar and cream butter well, until light and fluffy. Sieve flour and salt together and stir into creamed mixture. Add finely chopped almonds and candied orange peel and mix well. Finally stir in the milk. Place teaspoons (1 x 5ml) of the mixture on a lightly buttered baking tray spacing them at least 2in (5cm) apart to allow plenty of room for them to spread during cooking. Flatten each spoonful gently with a wet fork. Bake in a moderately hot oven (400°F, 200°C; Gas Mark 6) for 6–8 minutes. Remove from the oven and leave to cool on the baking tray for 3–4 minutes to harden. Remove with a palette knife and leave to get cold on a wire rack. Store in an airtight tin.

Shortbread Hearts *(makes 24–30)*

8oz (225g) unsalted butter	8oz (225g) plain flour
4oz (125g) caster sugar	4oz (125g) cornflour

Cream together the butter and sugar. Gradually work in the sieved flour and cornflour to form a dough. Knead until smooth. Roll out on a lightly floured board to a thickness of about 1/4in (6mm). Cut out with a heart-shaped cutter. Place on a buttered baking tray, leaving room for the biscuits to expand. Bake towards the top of a moderate oven (325°F, 160°C; Gas Mark 3) for 15–20 minutes or until lightly brown. Sprinkle with caster sugar while still warm, but leave for a few minutes to harden before removing from the baking tray. Cool on a wire rack and store in an airtight container until needed.

Variations:
Ginger Shortbread Hearts
Sieve 2 teaspoons (2 x 5ml) ground ginger with the flour.

Orange Shortbread Hearts
Add grated rind of 2 oranges to butter and sugar mixture.

Almond Shortbread Hearts
Add 3oz (75g) ground almonds to butter and sugar mixture, and almond essence to taste.

Sponge Fingers *(makes about 20)*

3 eggs, separated	2–3 drops vanilla essence
3oz (75g) caster sugar	Sieved icing sugar for sprinkling
3 1/2 oz (90g) plain flour	

Line 2 large baking trays with lightly greased greaseproof or Bakewell paper. Place egg yolks and sugar in a mixing bowl and beat together until thick and pale in colour. Whisk egg whites stiffly and fold gently into the egg-yolk mixture with sieved flour and vanilla essence. Using a piping bag fitted with a plain 1/2in (1cm) nozzle, pipe mixture in 3in (7 1/2 cm) lengths on the prepared baking trays. Sprinkle with sieved icing sugar and bake near the top of a moderate oven (350°F, 180°C; Gas Mark 4) for about 10 minutes or until pale brown in colour. When cooked, remove biscuits from baking trays and cool on a wire tray. Store in an airtight tin until wanted.

INDEX

126